A Postcard View of Hell
One Doughboy's Souvenir Album of the First World War

Frank Jacob
Nord University, Norway

Mark D. Van Ells
Queensborough Community College (CUNY)

Series in Critical Media Studies

Copyright © 2019 Vernon Press, an imprint of Vernon Art and Science Inc, on behalf of the author.

All rights reserved. No part of this publication may be reproduced, stored in a retrieval system, or transmitted in any form or by any means, electronic, mechanical, photocopying, recording, or otherwise, without the prior permission of Vernon Art and Science Inc.

www.vernonpress.com

In the Americas:
Vernon Press
1000 N West Street,
Suite 1200, Wilmington,
Delaware 19801
United States

In the rest of the world:
Vernon Press
C/Sancti Espiritu 17,
Malaga, 29006
Spain

Series in Critical Media Studies

Library of Congress Control Number: 2018953599

ISBN: 978-1-62273-673-7

Also available:

Hardback: 978-1-62273-451-1

E-book: 978-1-62273-595-2

Product and company names mentioned in this work are the trademarks of their respective owners. While every care has been taken in preparing this work, neither the authors nor Vernon Art and Science Inc. may be held responsible for any loss or damage caused or alleged to be caused directly or indirectly by the information contained in it.

Every effort has been made to trace all copyright holders, but if any have been inadvertently overlooked the publisher will be pleased to include any necessary credits in any subsequent reprint or edition.

Cover image by Frank Marhefka, "Firing a Heavy C.A.C."
Cover design by Vernon Press using elements designed by aopsan / Freepik.

Table of Contents

Preface — v

Introduction: The Postcard and the Great War — ix

Chapter 1 **The World of Frank Marhefka** — 1

Chapter 2 **Frank Marhefka's Postcard Collection** — 17

Epilogue — 127

Works Cited — 131

Index — 141

Preface

Picture postcards are such common things in today's world that most people rarely think about them. People send postcards to keep in touch with friends and relatives while they are on vacation, or collect them as keepsakes of their travels. They often end up in garbage cans or recycling bins, but sometimes they find their way into archival collections; and for those who look at them carefully, postcards can offer valuable insights into the time periods in which they were created, and the mentalities of those who bought or sent them. As historians of the military experience, we found ourselves interested in one particular postcard collection, bound in an album and now held in the archives of the Northumberland County Historical Society in Sunbury, Pennsylvania. It is a souvenir not of a vacation, but of war. The album was the property of an American soldier from Northumberland County named Frank Marhefka, who served in France during the First World War, during which he collected postcards that offer insight into several different dimensions of the war, ranging from new technologies to the total destruction they brought upon buildings and soldiers' lives alike. Inspecting Marhefka's postcards, we believed that these seemingly ordinary objects, collected by an ordinary soldier, had something to say.

Marhefka's postcards raised two interconnected lines of questions in our minds. First, what can these images tell us about the nature of the First World War experience? His images show the hard realities of war, such as battle scenes, and the destruction left in the wake of the fighting. Occasionally the images are quite gruesome, depicting the dead – their bodies twisted and distorted – individually and in groups. More common are images of the military equipment, including tanks, airplanes, artillery pieces, that created such destruction. However, there are also portraits of political and military leaders, as well as photos of scenes behind the lines. Some images come from the Allied side of the conflict, others from the German. Though the United States did not enter the war until 1917, Marhefka's postcards span the entirety of the conflict. Presented with commentary, we surmised, this collection could offer an instructive tutorial on the world of the Great War soldier – a walk through the conflict as the fighting man saw it.

The second line of questions had to do with the role of postcards in the lives of soldiers. Marhefka was hardly alone in collecting them during the Great War. Any historian who has done research on that conflict has undoubtedly been impressed with the sheer number of postcards in soldiers' archival collections. They are frequently interspersed among letters home. Many of the troops, like Marhefka, gathered them up and placed them in albums. Sometimes there are scrapbooks chock full of photographs and other bits of ephemera as well as postcards. In their research, most historians read the written messages on these cards, but likely give little thought to the images on the other side. However, Great War soldiers were communicating through the imagery on the postcards too. Why was the postcard such a strongly favored form of communication for the soldiers of the First World War? Who produced these wartime postcards, and where did soldiers acquire them? What kinds of postcards were available to the soldiers? What were Marhefka and other Great War soldiers trying to say about their wartime experience by sending and collecting these picture postcards?

What follows is an attempt to weave together such questions, and in the process shed light on a little examined and underappreciated aspect of the social and cultural world of First World War soldiers. An introductory text outlines the history of the modest little postcard and explores its significance during the Great War. Chapter One gives a biographical sketch of Frank Marhefka, from his humble beginnings in a Pennsylvania coal mining town to his journey to France to serve in the war. Chapter Two consists of the postcards themselves. Here we offer commentary on the images, putting them into historical context and suggesting further reading. Though our study is built around one particular soldier – an American – the lives of soldiers are strikingly similar from army to army. We, therefore, place Marhefka's collection into a larger narrative of World War I military experience that goes beyond national borders.

A century after the conclusion of the "the war to end all wars," the Frank Marhefka postcard collection offers vivid and valuable insights into the First World War, in that it tells the stories, through pictures, that soldiers were often reluctant to discuss in their letters, memoirs, and oral histories. Marhefka collected these images as a souvenir of his journey through that war, and his images offer a disturbing yet fascinating "postcard view of hell."

***

The authors would like to thank the following people for their vital contributions to making this work possible: Belinda Albright, Roger Alleman, Riccardo Altieri, John Haile, Tonie Holt, Cindy Inkrote, Manfred Jacob, Jack Lindermuth, Alan Petroulis, Paula Van Ells, and Eric Van Slander. In addition, we would also like to thank the archivists, librarians and staff members at the following institutions: the Croton Free Library, the Kurt Schmeller Library at Queensborough Community College, the Mount Carmel Library, the National Archives, the Northumberland County Historical Society, the Shamokin Public Library, the Sunbury Public Library, and the Library of Würzburg University, Germany.

Introduction:
The Postcard and the Great War

Deltiologists (those who study and collect postcards) refer to the first two decades of the twentieth century as the "Golden Age" of the postcard. "'Postcarditis' has made its appearance in nearly every city and town [in] America with a vengeance," claimed one postcard enthusiast in 1907. "Thousands are afflicted with the disease and more are afflicted each day... Statistics from abroad indicate the same conditions. There is scarcely a store in any city or town that does not display those little squares of pasteboard."[1] The First World War broke out at the height of the postcard craze, and for millions around the world those "little squares of pasteboard" greatly shaped the way they understood that titanic conflict. Indeed, "postcarditis" particularly affected soldiers[2] of the Great War, whether they were a British Tommy, a French *poilu*, an American doughboy, a German "*boche*"[3] or an Ottoman "Mehmet." These ordinary little objects offered them a connection to home, amusement, and they could even be badges of honor. The examination of World War I postcards offers a revealing glimpse into the mentality of the soldiers, the way the soldiers viewed the war, and the way they wanted the rest of the people, who had stayed behind the front, to understand their world.

The Golden Age of the Postcard

The origins of the postcard are murky, but can be found with the postal reforms of the mid-nineteenth century. Britain's Uniform Penny Post, implemented in 1840, ushered in the era of postage stamps and low uniform rates. Though these reforms made sending letters less expensive and

---

[1] Arthur L. Shaver, "Postcarditis Is Now Prevalent," *The Philatelic West* 35, 3 (February 28, 1907): n.p.

[2] For the purposes of this study, the term "soldier" is used generically for all military personnel, including those serving in naval and air forces.

[3] French soldiers would refer to their German enemies as "boche," usually used to describe Germans in a negative way. The word per se means stubborn or boneheaded.

more efficient, some saw further opportunities for simplification and advocated doing away with the envelope altogether. The first known postcard dates to Britain in 1840, when a playwright named Theodore Hook (1788-1841) mailed a card to himself with an image of buffoonish postal workers gathered around an inkwell. It is unclear what kind of statement Hook (a known practical joker) was trying to make. "While Hook clearly was an unusual person," claimed postcard historian Edward Proud, "it also seems that he was responsible for one of the greatest Victorian inventions."[4] Hook's card was a novelty, but in the 1860s postcards came into more common use. In 1861, an American printer named John P. Charlton copyrighted a postcard and went into business with a colleague named Hymen Lipman (1817-1893) to produce them. The "Lipman Postal Card" was made of cardboard, and had a blank front side for the message, while on the reverse showed lines for the recipient's address and a box for the stamp, as well as a decorative border. Similar innovations occurred in Europe. When Prussian postal reformer Heinrich von Stephan (1831-1897) first discussed the possibility of a postcard in 1865, his ideas were not met with much enthusiasm.[5] However, based on a proposal by Vienna economist Emanuel Hermann (1839-1902), the Austrian postal service in 1869 debuted what it called the "Correspondenz Karte" (Correspondence Card), a government-issued card with prepaid postage already embossed on it.[6]

Postcards soon spread to and across Europe. The U.S. Post Office issued its own penny postcards with prepaid postage in 1873. In the first seven weeks of their availability, the post office sold 31 million of them.[7] Some countries, like Britain, initially tried to maintain a state monopoly on postcards, but publishers like Raphael Tuck & Sons, recognizing their commercial potential, protested such a policy.[8] By the mid-1880s, it had

---

[4] "Historic Postcard Sells for Pounds 27,000," *Times of London*, March 9, 2002.

[5] Klaus Beyrer, ed. *Kommunikation im Kaiserreich: Der Generalpostmeister Heinrich von Stephan* (Heidelberg: Edition Braus, 1997). Ironically, the German Post published a memorial postcard when Stephan died in 1897. See Postkarte zum Tod von Heinrich von Stephan, Verlag Keltz und Meiners, 1897, Deutsches Historisches Museum, Objektdatenbank, PK 2014/2979. Stephan's idea was rejected, because the responsible Prussian officials considered an open message to be too immoral and probably offensive.

[6] Robert Lebeck and Gerhard Kaufmann, *Viele Grüße...: Eine Kulturgeschichte der Postkarte* (Dortmund: Harenberg, 1985), 401.

[7] Winifred Gallagher, *How the Post Office Created America: A History* (New York: Penguin, 2016), 212-213.

[8] John Fraser, "Propaganda on the Picture Postcard," *Oxford Art Journal* 3, 2 (1980), *Propaganda*: 39.

become legal to mail privately produced cards internationally. Advances in printing technology in the late nineteenth century allowed for increasingly elaborate and colorful images, though this reduced the space available to write a message. However, in 1907 the Universal Postal Union authorized the divided back postcard. On such cards, the reverse side had two sections. The left half was reserved for writing a brief message, while the right half was for the recipient's address and the stamp – allowing for the front of the card to be taken up entirely by an image.[9]

As the twentieth century dawned, a postcard craze gripped the West and then the world. The new medium had its critics. As German media studies scholar Anett Holzheid noted, some believed the postcard to be a technological regression as compared to the telegram — and, due to its mass use, considered it a lowbrow form of communication as well.[10] Others raised privacy concerns, since postal officials would be able to read the messages written on them, though as Irish postcard historian Séamus Kearns suggested, the sheer number of circulated postcards made it impossible for the officials to read all the messages.[11] Despite such criticisms, the popularity of the postcard could not be restrained. The postcard provided, as Anett Holzheid emphasized, a "timely simplification of written communication" that combined "the assets of the cost intensive and as exclusive connotated telegram … with the habitualized use of the comparatively cheap letter."[12] But for turn-of-the-century consumers, it was rather the rich, vibrant imagery that gave postcards their greatest appeal. Austrian historian Joachim Bürgschwentner characterized them as an "important visual media" that allowed people "to 'get a picture' of events or loca-

---

[9] For more on the history and evolution of the postcard, see Fraser, "Propaganda"; Séamus Kearns, "Picture Postcards As A Source For Social Historians," *Saothar* 22 (1997): 128-133; Lebeck and Kaufmann, *Viele Grüße*; Otto May, *Deutsch sein heißt treu sein: Ansichtskarten als Spiegel von Mentalität und Untertanerziehung in der wilhelminischen Ära (1888–1918)* (Hildesheim: Lax, 1998); David Prochaska and Jordan Mendelson, eds., *Postcards: Ephemeral Histories of Modernity* (University Park, PA: Pennsylvania State University Press, 2010); Bjarne Rogan, "An Entangled Object: The Picture Postcard as Souvenir and Collectible, Exchange and Ritual Communication," *Cultural Analysis* 4 (2005): 1-27; Dorothy B. Ryan, *Picture Postcards in the United States, 1893-1918*, updated edition (New York: Clarkson N. Potter, 1982); and Martin Willoughby, *A History of Postcards: A Pictorial Record from the Turn of the Century to the Present Day* (London: Bracken Books, 1994).
[10] Anett Holzheid, *Das Medium Postkarte: Eine sprachwissenschaftliche und mediengeschichtliche Studie* (Berlin: Erich Schmidt Verlag, 2011), 10-11.
[11] Kearns, "Picture Postcards," 130.
[12] Holzheid, *Medium*, 9.

tions."[13] "Immediate visual attraction," wrote art historian John Fraser, "gave the postcard a much wider range of purchasers."[14] Given their ubiquity at the turn of the twentieth century, postcards offer a rich and revealing resource for linguistic, cultural, or semiotic studies at the dawn of the twentieth century.[15]

Advertisers were among the first to recognize the advantages of the postcard, but soon millions found other uses for them. The postcard was (and still is) most commonly thought of as a souvenir of a particular event or of one's travels. "The picture postcard is the universal souvenir," wrote U.S author Frank Stefano, Jr. "It is the one that is bought in all places by everyone, even those who otherwise never indulge the souvenir instinct," and is often "found in spots that carry no other souvenir items."[16] Postcards were popular mementoes of the numerous world fairs and exhibitions in the *fin de siècle* period, such as the Paris Universal Exposition of 1889 (from which many cards bore the image of the brand new Eiffel Tower), Britain's Royal Naval Exhibition of 1891, and the World's Columbian Exposition in Chicago in 1893. Postcards were perhaps most commonly associated with the growing tourist trade. By 1900, visitors to virtually every city or attraction of note in Europe or North America (and even beyond) could purchase postcards with drawings or photographs of that location's street scenes and landmarks – which typically included the words "Greetings from" of "Souvenir of" that location. "Tourists grabbed them from the racks at roadside stops, hotels, and boardwalks," wrote historian Robert Bogdan and librarian Todd Weseloh "to show, tell and document their adventures."[17]

But the significance of postcards went far beyond their souvenir value. They came in endless varieties. Many illustrators, painters, and photographers saw the postcard as a new outlet for their work. The British firm Raphael Tuck & Sons commissioned painters to produce several series of "*oilettes*" – paintings depicting rural and village themes. In Vienna, a struggling artist named Adolf Hitler (1889-1945) peddled his work in post-

---

[13] Joachim Bürgschwentner, "War Relief, Patriotism and Art: The State-Run Production of Picture Postcards in Austria1914–1918," *Austrian Studies* 21 (2013), *Cultures at War: Austria-Hungary 1914–1918*, 101.

[14] Fraser, "Propaganda," 39

[15] Holzheid, *Medium*, 27. For an introduction to semiotics, see: Daniel Chandler, *Semiotics: The Basics*, 2nd edition (New York: Routledge, 2007).

[16] Frank Stefano, Jr., *Pictorial Souvenirs and Commemoratives of North America* (New York: E.P. Dutton, 1976), 122.

[17] Robert Bodgan and Todd Weseloh, *Real Photo Postcard Guide: The People's Photography* (Syracuse, NY: Syracuse University Press, 2006). 2.

card form. Postcards also had political dimensions. They spread the idea of the nation by establishing a sphere of communication,[18] as well as a group identity or an imagined community[19] at the same time.[20] This means that postcards as a cheaper format for a more general exchange of ideas widened the sphere of communication of the national community as such, but also helped this community to imagine itself better by spreading images that helped to identify the idea of the nation, as well as its physical and legal expression, i.e. the nation state. Images of historical events, heroic ancestors, famous politicians, but also maps and other depictions of national values, e.g. legends and fairy tales, helped to create a strong nationalist feeling towards their own belonging to the modern nation states. The postcard consequently also helped to invent national traditions and circulated their visualization to the masses.[21]

The public often followed politics and global affairs through postcards, though as political scientist Jon D. Carlson noted, they often presented news events as a form of entertainment. Eye-catching images and brief texts, he argues, appealed to the "middle to lower classes in a newly-emerging semiliterate urban population" that was a major consumer of the medium. Military conflicts, like the Russo-Japanese War of 1904-1905, offered a particularly heady blend of dramatic events combined with compelling visual images that captured the imagination of a population that might not normally follow global events very closely. "Like modern infotainment," Carlson wrote, postcards brought "foreign policy issues to the attention of an otherwise inattentive public, often as a 'byproduct' of their use."[22]

Postcards usually served more mundane purposes. There were postcards with the visages of singers, dancers, athletes, and other celebrities. The emerging film industry began publishing promotional postcards of fa-

---

[18] Karl W. Deutsch, *Nationalism and Social Communication: An Inquiry Into the Foundations of Nationality* (Cambridge, MA: MIT Press, 1953). The postcard as a new medium of exchange had also stimulated a "trend of short communication." Holzheid, *Medium*, 9.

[19] Benedict Anderson, *Imagined Communities: Reflections on the Origin and Spread of Nationalism*, revised edition (London: Verso, 2016).

[20] Otto May, *Deutsch sein heißt treu sein*.

[21] Eric J. Hobsbawm and Terence Ranger, eds. *The Invention of Tradition* (Cambridge: Cambridge University Press, 1983).

[22] Jon D. Carlson, "Postcards and Propaganda: Postcards as Soft News Images of the Russo-Japanese War," *Political Communication* 26 (2009): 212-237.

mous actors.[23] One could send a postcard to offer birthday or holiday greetings. According to historian Daniel Gifford, holiday postcards in the United States were particularly popular with rural white women of Anglo-Saxon or Germanic heritage from the northern states, and often expressed their concerns about gender roles and social change during the Progressive Era.[24] Some provided religious inspiration, others sexual titillation. Indeed, historian Lisa Z. Sigel notes that the postcard significantly hastened the transformation of pornography from "literary to visual" outlets, and made it available to a much wider audience."[25] Publishers on both sides of the Atlantic issued cards of blatantly racist caricatures as a form of amusement, such as "coon cards" in the United States, which portrayed African Americans in demeaning and stereotypical ways.[26] "The list of subjects," claimed John Fraser, "could be extended almost indefinitely."[27] There were scores of novelty cards. Some were made of leather or wood. Some featured birds with real feathers glued onto them, or portraits with real hair. "There were hundreds of different types available, with hundreds of different reasons for sending them," wrote postcard historian Martin Willoughby:

> Postcards depicting birthday or Christmas greetings, actresses, ships, railway engines, animals, military leaders, and the works of leading artists began to appear in shops… Soon a person did not need a particular reason to send a postcard to a friend – the picture was reason enough, and if you were lucky, the recipient might send one in return.[28]

---

[23] Q. David Bowers, "Souvenir Postcards and the Development of the Star System, 1912-1914," *Film History* 3 (1989): 39-45.

[24] Daniel Gifford, *American Holiday Postcards, 1905-1915: Imagery and Context* (Jefferson, NC: McFarland, 2013).

[25] Lisa Z. Sigel, "Filth in the Wrong People's Hands: Postcards and the Expansion of Pornography in Britain and the Atlantic World, 1880-1914," *Journal of Social History* 33, 4 (2000): 859-885.

[26] JBHE Foundation, "'Coon Cards': Racist Postcards Have Become Collectors' Items," *Journal of Blacks in Higher Education* 25 (1999): 72-73; Wayne M. Mellinger, "Postcards from the Edge of the Color Line: Images of African Americans in Popular Culture," *Symbolic Interaction* 15, 4 (1992): 413-433.

[27] Fraser, "Propaganda,", 39.

[28] Willoughby, *A History of Postcards*, 10.

Introduction

British sociologists Tonie and Valmai Holt characterized postcards as "Victorian television"[29] – an observation equally cogent for the Edwardian period immediately preceding the First World War. In the days before social media, email, or even the widespread use of the telephone, the postcard was an ideal form for passing on pleasantries, humor, and tidbits of news and information. They were the memes, tweets, and Facebook posts of the early twentieth century.

Germany was the undisputed king of postcard production. The German industry centered on Dresden and Leipzig, where firms such as Meisner & Buch and Stengel dominated the business. Gustav Liersch and Photochrom, based in Berlin, expanded into English-language markets, while the Neue Photographische Gesellschaft established a subsidiary outside Paris at Saint-Denis to tap into the Francophone world.[30] Entrepreneurs in other countries soon followed the German example and established their own corporations, such as Munk (Austria), Traldi (Italy), De Rycker & Mendel (Belgium), and Photoglob (Switzerland). American companies increasingly got in on the action, such as the Detroit Publishing Company, Leighton & Valentine, and the Souvenir Post Card Company, just to name a few. Many U.S. companies had German connections, such as Curt Teich & Company, founded by a German immigrant in Chicago in 1898, and the E.C. Kropp Company of Milwaukee. Kropp went into the postcard business after "visiting his old home in Germany" where, according to his obituary in the *American Stationer*, he "saw the popularity of the post card there and saw the possibilities of the fad in this country." By the time of his death in 1907, the E.C. Kropp Company had produced an estimated 20 million postcards.[31]

By the first decade of the twentieth century, the world experienced a flood of postcards of near-biblical proportions. In 1906, Germany produced just over one billion picture postcards. The United States ranked second with 770 million, followed by Great Britain with 734 million.[32] In

---

[29] Tonie and Valmai Holt, *Till the Boys Come Home: The First World War Through Its Picture Postcards*, updated edition (Barnsley: Pen and Sword, 2014), 8.

[30] Wilma Gütgemann-Holtz and Wolfgang Holtz, ed. *Neue Photographische Gesellschaft Steglitz: Die Geschichte eines Weltunternehmens* (Berlin: n.p., 2009). Photographs became an example of the amalgamation of a new technology with the new medium of the picture postcard. See: Ludwig Hoerner, Das photographische Gewerbe in Deutschland, 1839-1914 (Düsseldorf: GFW-Verlag, 1989), 84-87; Karin Walter, Postkarte und Fotografie: Studien zur Massenbild-Produktion (Würzburg: Bayerische Blätter für Volkskunde, 1995), 23-26.

[31] "Obituary, Emil C. Kropp," *American Stationer* 63, 1 (1908): 22.

[32] Lebeck and Kaufmann, *Viele Grüße...*, 418.

1913, Germany still ranked first with 1.7 billion, followed by Japan with 1.3 billion, and Great Britain with around 900 million sold picture postcards.[33] The number of postcards printed and mailed was staggering. "Roughly speaking," wrote Norwegian historian Bjarne Rogan, "between 200 and 300 billion postcards were produced and sold during this Golden Age."[34]

Consumers typically bought postcards at places like newsstands or drug and department stores, but there were also shops dedicated exclusively to postcards. After arriving in Chicago, a German immigrant named Otto Koehn noticed that "there were no post-card shops as there were in the old country, and I saw that this field was new and untried in America." Koehn saved his money, made connections with wholesalers, and opened his own postcard shop soon after his arrival in the Windy City. His business struggled at first, but as he learned about American tastes his profits grew, and he soon expanded his operations. "I started another store," he said. "Then I started another store, and then another, and then three more." By 1912, the *Dry Good Reporter* noted that Koehn's chain of postcard shops earned him enough money "to pay $20,000 a year rent for store buildings, buy a residence and an automobile, all in the six and a half years he has been in America."[35] There were even postcard vending machines. In Springfield, Illinois, a drug store owner developed one that could offer up to 500 cards. The customer turned a handle to view the cards individually. "When a card appears which suits the fancy of the operator," explained the *Dry Goods Reporter*, "he drops a coin into a coin slot and then turns the handle again and the selected card is fed out at the front of the machine."[36]

In addition to the countless varieties of postcards that streamed out of publishing houses, people could make their own. The development of photography in the nineteenth century had a major impact on the evolution of the postcard. In the early days of the medium, photography was only for a small group of skilled specialists, usually working out of a studio. "Access to the specialized and complex technology of photography required time, money and scientific background," wrote art professor Bob Rogers, "so that popular participation was limited to having one's portrait

---

[33] Fraser, "Propaganda," 39.
[34] Rogan, "An Entangled Object," 1.
[35] "Successful Retailer of Postcards," *Dry Goods Reporter*, 42, 21 (May 25, 1912): 40.
[36] "Druggist Invents Post-Card Machine," *Dry Goods Reporter* 42, 4 (27 January 1912): 51.

Introduction xvii

taken."³⁷ However, by the end of the century photography had effectively been democratized. The Eastman Kodak Company of Rochester, New York led the way in the developing cameras for personal use. "Freed from the structures of the studio," wrote librarian Greg Kocken, now "the photo enthusiast could pursue casual shots in more public settings ... [and] amateur photographers became chroniclers of everyday life, from their own intimate circles of friends and family to individuals in the wider community, with the studio backdrop replaced by the environs of home, the public sphere, and the natural world."³⁸

Kodak greatly influenced the Golden Age of postcards with the introduction of the Model 3A Folding Pocket Camera in 1903 – the first so-called "postcard camera." Film from such cameras was developed directly onto stiff postcard paper, with the address and message sections already pre-printed on the reverse, creating what collectors today know as a "real photo" postcard. Many postcard camera models included a window on the camera through which the photographer could etch onto the negative captions and notes about the images they had captured. Thanks to the real picture postcard, travelers could not just send a picture postcard *of* Paris, but one with a photograph of them *in* Paris. Real photo postcards were usually printed in small batches – from fewer than a dozen to several hundred – though they could be mass produced as well. Real photo postcards tended to focus on everyday slices of life – street scenes, local landmarks, disasters and other newsworthy events. In the United States – especially in the South – local photographers captured scenes of lynchings and printed up souvenir postcards of these macabre events. From their colonial empires abroad, Europeans often sent home postcards that captured the perceived exoticism, backwardness, and savagery of those they ruled.³⁹

---

³⁷ Bob Rogers, "Photography and the Photographic Image," *Art Journal* 38, 1 (1978): 30.
³⁸ Greg Kocken, "The Amateur's Eye: Daniel Bastian Nelson in Eau Claire," *Wisconsin Magazine of History* 101, 2 (2018): 29-30.
³⁹ For more on real photo postcards, see Bogdan and Weseloh, *Real Photo Postcard Guide*; Luc Sante, *Folk Photography: The American Real-Photo Postcard* (Portland, OR: Verse Chorus Press, 2009); Rosamond B. Vaule, *As We Were: American Photographic Postcards, 1905-1930* (Boston: David R. Godine, 2004); Laetitia Wolff, ed., *Real Photo Postcards: Unbelievable Images from the Collection of Harvey Tulcensky* (Princeton, NJ: Princeton Architectural Press, 2005). For more on lynching postcards, see James Allen, Hilton Als, Congressman John Lewis, and Leon F. Litwack, *Without Sanctuary: Lynching Photography in America* (Santa Fe, NM: Twin Palms Publishers, 2000).

Postcards were, however, not just a method of communication. They were also collectible. Like stamps, dolls, coins, spoons, pins, baseball cards, or countless other such things, millions of people collected postcards. Even Britain's Queen Victoria (1819-1901) famously kept a collection. The pursuit of "philocarty" or "cartephilia" – as the love of postcards was then known – involved various accoutrements. Postcard retailers peddled a great variety of albums in which to store the cards. Some were simple, with canvas covers and die-cut slits on paper pages to hold the cards. Others could be quite elaborate, bound in wood or fine leather. "It seemed as if every American home had a postcard album on the parlor table," wrote art historian Rosamond Vaule, who also noted that "the album's role went beyond domestic entertainment and the preservation of precious souvenirs and family history." These albums, which could display one's tastes in art of the extent of one's travels, "also conveyed social standing and sophistication, depending on the quality and origin of the postcard contents."[40]

There were other ways to share one's collection. The Bausch & Lomb Company of Rochester, New York – noted for the manufacture of eyeglasses – introduced the "Reflectoscope Post Card Magic Lantern" in 1909, allowing the collector to project his or her cards on a screen. Thousands joined postcard collecting clubs. Members not only disseminated information about the latest trends in the industry, but also exchanged cards so that individuals could build their collections. *The Gregg Writer*, an American magazine dedicated to shorthand, organized a club whose members exchanged cards written exclusively in that script. Some clubs, like the Union Souvenir Card Exchange, had an international membership, in which people would typically swap views of their home communities. "I have received cards from Europe, Asia, Africa, Australia, and every civilized country in the world," wrote club member Arthur Shaver, who claimed to have met members "who have collected from 1000 to 300,000 each." Collecting and exchanging postcards "has a valuable educational side as well as being a pleasure and a token of friendship," claimed Shaver. "Friends living far apart may become acquainted, to a certain extent at least, with each other's surroundings through an exchange of cards."[41]

The Postcard Goes to War

Whatever global amity postcard collecting may have created, it did not save humanity from the First World War. The Great War is usually referred

---

[40] Vaule, *As We Were*, 50-60.

[41] Shaver, "Postcarditis," n.p.

Introduction

to as the "seminal catastrophe"[42] of the twentieth century, ending of the "long" nineteenth century[43] and beginning of the century of extremes.[44] Almost the entirety of Europe went to war. This titanic conflict pitted the Central Powers (Germany, Austria, and the Ottoman Empire and later Bulgaria) against the Allies (Britain, France, Russia, and later Italy and the United States). After years of rising German-American tensions, the United States joined the Allies in 1917. Machine guns and modern artillery, mass-produced and in the hands of mass armies, made the First World War the bloodiest conflict Western Civilization had ever seen. The Western Front, known for its trench war, also confronted the soldiers with a totally new war experience, far away from the romantic image of a heroic fight between gentlemen. Pure destruction, a "no-man's-land" that could hardly be crossed alive, and an immanent perception of death around oneself were the determinant factors of this war. A postcard, in this melancholic environment, linked the soldiers to home, a better world far away from their daily routine of destruction.[45] On the Eastern Front, the lines seesawed back and forth indecisively, but it was the trench warfare on the Western Front where the war reached perhaps its most brutal dimensions. Armies on both sides hammered away at each other futilely. Millions died in a new kind of mechanized slaughter, yet the front lines barely budged. For the soldiers in the trenches, life seemed apocalyptic. Mud, fleas, and rats were their constant companions, and the smell of death hung constantly in the air. When there was no fighting, boredom ruled.[46]

---

[42] George F. Kennan, *The Decline of Bismarck's European Order: Franco-Russian Relations, 1875-1890* (Princeton, NJ: Princeton University Press, 1979), 3.

[43] Franz J. Bauer, *Das "lange" 19. Jahrhundert (1789-1917): Profil einer Epoche* (Stuttgart: Reclam, 2004).

[44] Eric Hobsbawm, *The Age of Extremes: A History of the World, 1914-1991* (New York: Vintage Books, 1996).

[45] On the experience of the new dimension of the Great War, especially with regard to the larger material battles in 1916, see Christian Stachelbeck, ed. *Materialschlachten 1916: Ereignis, Bedeutung, Erinnerung* (Paderborn: Ferdinand Schöningh, 2017).

[46] Stephen Bull, *Trench: A History of Trench Warfare on the Western Front* (London: Osprey, 2014).

In all combatant nations, postcard production thrived despite rigid economic regimentation.[47] Postcards had a great many wartime uses. Governments of warring nations quickly repurposed them for propaganda. The picture postcard was an "ideal vehicle for propaganda," wrote John Fraser, since it was "cheap, easy to handle, with an instant visual appeal so that it was easily appreciated, more particularly by those who were illiterate."[48] Governments issued postcards, along with posters and other visual media, to promote war bond drives or for other war-related purposes. However, propaganda ministries rarely published postcards themselves. Rather, governments typically worked with relief organizations and commercial manufacturers, making government photographs or the works of official war artists available to them, in their efforts to boost home front morale.[49]

Indeed, as independent scholar Christine Brocks astutely noted, the wishes and desires of consumers were still the primary drivers of wartime

---

[47] For more on postcards and the First World War, see Christine Brocks, *Die bunte Welt des Krieges: Bildpostkarten aus dem Ersten Weltkrieg 1914-1918* (Essen: Klartext Verlag, 2008); Elena S. Danielson, "Russian and German Great War Postcards," *Slavic and Eastern European Information Resources* 17, 3 (2016): 151-164; Guus de Vries, *The Great War through Picture Postcards* (Barnsley: Pen & Sword Books, 2016); Thomas Flemming and Ulf Heinrich, *Grüße aus dem Schützengraben: Feldpostkarten im Ersten Weltkrieg* (Berlin: be.bra, 2004); Holt and Holt, *Till the Boys Come Home*; John Laffin, *World War I in Postcards* (Gloucester: Alan Sutton, 1988); Elisabeth von Hagenow, "Mit Gott für König, Volk und Vaterland: Die Bildpostkarte als Massen- und Bekenntnismedium," in *Bildpropaganda im Ersten Weltkrieg*, ed. Raoul Zühlke (Hamburg: Verlag Ingrid Kämpfer, 2000), 145. The collection at the German Historical Museum also provides an interesting insight into the wide portfolio of existing German picture postcards during the war period. Deutsches Historisches Museum, *Der Erste Weltkrieg in deutschen Bildpostkarten*, CD-Rom (Berlin: Directmedia Publ., 2004).

[48] Fraser. "Propaganda,"42.

[49] For more on postcards and propaganda during the First World War, see Bürgschwentner, "War Relief"; Christine Brocks, "Der Krieg auf der Postkarte: Feldpostkarten im ersten Weltkrieg," in *Der Tod als Maschinist: Der industrialisierte Krieg 1914–1918*, eds. Rolf Spilker and Bernd Ulrich (Bramsche: Rasch, 1998), 154-163; Oskar Dohle and Andrea Weiß, "'Österreich wird ewig stehn': Postkarten als Mittel der Propaganda in Österreich-Ungarn im Ersten Weltkrieg am Beispiel der Sammlung des Salzburger Landesarchivs," *Mitteilungen der Gesellschaft für Salzburger Landeskunde* 141 (2001): 293-324; Walter Lukan and Max Demeter Peyfuss, "Jeder Schuß ein Russ', jeder Stoß ein Franzos. Kriegspropaganda auf Postkarten 1914–1918," in *Jeder Schuss ein Russ — Jeder Stoss ein Franzos: Literarische und graphische Kriegspropaganda in Deutschland und Österreich 1914-1918*, eds. Hans Weigel, Walter Lukan and Max Demeter Peyfuss (Vienna: Brandstätter, 1983), 32-47.

Introduction xxi

postcard sales and distribution.[50] The public's desire for colorful and provocative imagery continued unabated after 1914, and with family members away in the services or working in war plants, the need for correspondence and connection with loved ones far away only grew. Indeed, John Fraser argued that World War I provided the postcard industry with another "great stimulus."[51] It is estimated that more than 50,000 different picture postcards were produced between 1914 and 1918 in Austria and Germany alone. All countries censored the mail during the war – texts as well as postcard images – though only a few kinds of images (extreme violence, pornography, etc.) were usually curtailed. The sheer number of postcards produced during the war is consequently amazing, and as Christine Brocks wrote, postcards "in their mass provide a sheer inexhaustible reservoir of the popular images" related to the war experience.[52]

Nationalistic themes were popular, at least during the early years of the war. Heads of state, from the German *kaiser* to the British king, made frequent appearances on wartime postcards, as did generals and war heroes. To promote the alliances, leaders from allied nations frequently appeared together on postcards, often with their national flags waving in dramatic and inspirational fashion in the background. Postcards sometimes portrayed the soldiers of enemy nations in negative caricatures. "German postcards like to show the French soldiers as sissies, the British as cowards and the Russians as unkempt, drunk, and full of lice," wrote Dutch historian Guus de Vries.[53] For their part, the Allies depicted the Germans as boorish and uncouth. Art cards remained popular, now repurposed for the war effort. Britain's Raphael Tuck & Sons put out a "European War" *oilette* series, for example. Some works were of notable quality. In Russia, the Tsarist government employed the artist Leonid Pasternak (1862-1945) to produce a series of postcard drawings for war relief that, according to archivist emerita Elena S. Danielson, were "realistic in an academic sense but marked by forthright individuality and understated intensity."[54] Many noted artists, now in uniform, produced works on postcards, such as French illustrator Ernest Gabard (1879-1957). His watercolors-turned-postcards intimately depicting life among the *poilus*, from camp life to combat operations, became bestsellers in France. Similarly, German artist Otto Dix (1891-1969) drew picture postcards that truthfully depicted war

---

[50] Brocks, *Die bunte Welt*, 237.
[51] Fraser, "Propaganda," 42.
[52] Brocks, *Die bunte Welt*, 11.
[53] de Vries, *The Great War through Picture Postcards*, 35.
[54] Danielson, "German and Russian Postcards," 162.

and the soldiers' own daily realities.⁵⁵ The kinds of images available on postcards were indeed inexhaustible. There were cards of women and children in military uniforms, relief organizations at work, sentimental farewells, and maps of the battlefronts. Some postcards contained patriotic music and poetry. There were photos and drawings of soldiers as well as their equipment, including airplanes, tanks, and machine guns. As the war dragged on and the jingoism of the early years faded, some postcards started to emphasize the costs of war. There were "images of grieving parents, spouses, and children at a soldier's grave," wrote de Vries, suggesting war weariness or even antiwar sentiments.⁵⁶

As in peacetime, the postcard was also a vehicle for keeping up with the news, and during the war the public was particularly hungry for information about their family members, friends, and neighbors at the front. Postcards gave the public visual images of the stories they read in the papers, and the folks back home eagerly gobbled them up. In Britain, for example, the government contracted with the newspaper *Daily Mail* to produce a series of postcards of official war photographs from the Western Front, with half the profits going to military charities. The first cards appeared after the Battle of the Somme in 1916, and were an instant hit with the public. Through postcards, the public could get a view of Tommy in action – albeit a selective one. The *Daily Mail* series was so popular with the British public that Tonie and Valmai Holt have gone so far as to argue that it was "the most popular series of cards ever produced in the history of postcards."⁵⁷

Across the Atlantic, Americans also followed the brutal events of the European war in part through postcard images. The *Chicago Daily News* published a popular series of photographic postcards from the battlefront. The *Daily News* was a pioneer among American newspapers in employing foreign correspondents, and when the war broke out its reporters and photographers documented the conflict for the American public. "Correspondents were hurried to the front to describe the war's earliest aspects," wrote Charles H. Dennis, the biographer of the paper's innovative publisher Victor Lawson (1850-1925), "mingling with the inhabitants of the cities and villages as the billows of steel rolled over them – presented by cable

---

⁵⁵ Dietrich Schubert, "Ein unbekanntes Kriegsbild von Otto Dix: Zur Frage der Abfolge seiner Kriegsarbeiten1915-1918," *Jahrbuch der Berliner Museen* 38 (1996): 152. For a detailed discussion of his war postcards, see Ulrike Rüdiger, *Grüsse aus dem Krieg: Die Feldpostkarten aus der Dix-Sammlung Gera* (Gera: Kunstgalerie Gera, 1991).

⁵⁶ de Vries, *The Great War through Picture Postcards*, 42.

⁵⁷ Holt and Holt, *Till the Boys Come Home*, 82.

intimate pictures of each day's startling events."⁵⁸ American public opinion about the war was mixed, and the postcard buying habits of Americans reflected those divisions. The 1915 sinking of the passenger ship *Lusitania* by a German submarine appeared on many postcards supporting the Allied cause. Pro-German postcards circulated too, especially among the nation's large German-American population. The magazine *Fatherland*, for example, published a series of postcards celebrating the 1916 visit of the German submarine *Deutschland* to Baltimore, which had successfully evaded the British naval blockade. "Take a set with you on your vacation and send them to your friends," the magazine urged its readers.⁵⁹ The overwhelming sentiment among Americans was to stay out of the conflict, and many postcards reflected neutral sentiments. The federal government wanted neutrality too, and feared inflammatory images might endanger it. In 1916, Postmaster General Albert S. Burleson (1863-1937) banned postcards and envelopes "of an unneutral nature" from the U.S. mail.

Once the United States joined the hostilities the following year, American publishers followed the lead of their European counterparts and spewed out scores of postcards with wartime themes to satisfy public demand. Some issued scenes from military training camps across the United States, featuring recruits engaged in a wide range of soldierly activities, from marching to firing weapons to preparing meals. With the arrival of American troops into the fighting, the Stars and Stripes often joined the Union Jack and the French Tricolor on countless postcards published on both sides of the Atlantic. In Italy in 1918, more than four million postcards were distributed for the purposes of propaganda, with images of American soldiers, John J. Pershing (1860-1948), the commander of the American Expeditionary Forces (AEF), and U.S. President Woodrow Wilson (1856-1924) prominently featured.⁶⁰

Military personnel were major consumers of wartime postcards. Soldiers themselves comprised what John Fraser called an "almost captive market,"⁶¹ though they are perhaps best seen as willing captives, since soldiers – like civilians – had a great many uses for postcards. The German Post

---

⁵⁸ Charles H. Dennis, *Victor Lawson: His Time and His Work* (Chicago: University of Chicago Press, 1935), 274.
⁵⁹ "The Blockade Runner," *The Fatherland: A Weekly* 5, 3 (August 23, 1916): 48.
⁶⁰ Fraser, "Propaganda," 42.
⁶¹ Ibid.

delivered 16.7 million field postcards, letters, and packages every day,[62] counting a total of 28.7 billion postal deliveries between August 1914 and November 1918. The French Post counted ten billion military postal deliveries during the war, averaging out at four million per day.[63]

In the Austrian case, 900,000 postcards were sent home from the front (or vice versa) every day.[64] Whether drawn, printed, or photographed, postcards from the wartime era underscore the various images the war prescribed to the soldiers. From these myriad images, writes Christine Brocks, the "mentalities, collective perceptions and interpretations" can be reconstructed and analyzed, and these images offer deep insight into the daily lives and experiences of the soldiers.[65]

First and foremost, postcards offered a quick and easy connection to home. Mail was exceptionally important to the men in the trenches. Homesick and in harm's way, soldiers were often desperate for any contact with home. Sending and receiving mail was also an important break from the monotony of war and offered a shred of normality in their lives.[66] Soldiers "wanted something to send to their loved ones at home at a time when letter writing was not always possible," wrote Martin Willoughby, and postcards "served as a cheering, quick method of communication in these difficult circumstances."[67] While the texts sent by soldiers were often monotonous, the images on the cards ranged from "sweet kitsch, through clumsy war propaganda and frivolous women in uniform, to realistic scenes of the everyday life at the front."[68] The banality of the texts could be owed to censorship, the soldiers' lack of writing capabilities or the fact that the postcards were more so signs of life than written expressions of art.[69] Postcards particularly suited poorly educated soldiers who found writing long letters challenging. "The soldiers liked the postcards," wrote Tonie

---

[62] 8.5 million of these postal deliveries consisted of postcards. Flemming and Heinrich, *Grüße aus dem Schützengraben*, 9.

[63] Ibid., 7-9.

[64] K. K. Handelsministerium, ed. *Statistik des österreichischen Post- und Telegraphenwesens im Jahre 1914* (Vienna, 1916), xv, cited in: Bürgschwentner, "War Relief," 102.

[65] Christine Brocks, *Die bunte Welt*, 12-14.

[66] Flemming and Heinrich, *Grüße aus dem Schützengraben*, 7.

[67] Willoughby, *A History of Postcards*, 110-111.

[68] Flemming and Heinrich, *Grüße aus dem Schützengraben*, 9.

[69] Ibid., 16.

Introduction

and Valmai Holt. "They were colorful and the pictures could often speak better for them than they could for themselves."[70]

Great War soldiers purchased a good many postcards not for communication, but as souvenirs. Men and women going off to war, like anyone else undertaking a journey, often pick up souvenirs to preserve the memories of their experiences. However, for military personnel souvenirs often have deeper meanings, highlighting their special status as veterans and as participants in great historical events.[71] Perhaps the most highly prized soldier mementos were enemy objects, symbolizing battlefield triumph. "The hunt for souvenirs was universal," wrote British author Richard Holmes of the British Tommy, "and prisoners and the fallen were routinely pillaged for cash and collectibles."[72] American doughboys were at least as voracious. Charles Elcock of the 28th Division recalled members of his unit seizing items from German prisoners during the Meuse-Argonne Offensive. "It was amusing to see the 'doughboys' rush at them with penknives," he wrote, "and rip their buttons off as souvenirs so that many of the poor devils had to hold their clothes together as they walked."[73] Some soldiers fashioned discarded shell casings and other military objects into commemorative vases, ashtrays, and other decorative items.[74] Military personnel also collected the same kinds of objects as peacetime tourists, including postcards. "The principal occupation of the boys here seems to be souvenirs," wrote American aviator Pat Crowe from the pilot training center at Saint-Maxient, France, and observed that "the first symptom of this dementia Americana is the acquisition of French Postcards."[75] Inex-

---

[70] Holt and Holt, *Till the Boys Come Home*, 9.

[71] Souvenir collecting by military personnel, despite its prevalence throughout the history of war, has received little scholarly attention. For more on the topic, see Mark D. Van Ells, "An Amazing Collection: American GIs and Their Souvenirs of World War II," in *War and Memorials: The Second World War and Beyond*, eds. Frank Jacob and Kenneth Pearl (Paderborn: Ferdinand Schöningh, forthcoming).

[72] Richard Holmes, *Tommy: The British Soldier on the Western Front, 1914-1918* (London: Harper Perennial, 2004), 546.

[73] James Henry Millar Andrews, Charles Elcock, and J.S. Bradford, *Soldiers of the Castle: A History of Company B, Engineer Battalion, National Guard of Pennsylvania, Afterward Company B, 103rd Engineers, 28th Division, A.E.F.* (Philadelphia: Hoeflich Printing House, 1929), 76.

[74] Artworks made by military personnel are known as "trench art." For an introduction to the genre, see Jane Kimball, *Trench Art: An Illustrated History* (Davis, CA: Silverpenny Press, 2004) and Nicholas J. Saunders, *Trench Art*, second edition (Barnsley: Pen & Sword, 2011).

[75] James Richard Crowe, *Pat Crowe, Aviator: Skylark Views and Letters from France* (New York: N.L. Brown, 1919), 57.

pensive, ubiquitous, and easy to store, postcards were for the soldier the perfect wartime souvenir.

Opportunities to collect postcards began immediately upon induction into the military. Local merchants swarmed around army posts and naval bases hoping to cash in on the military trade, postcards among their many wares. Many troops served in rear areas well behind the front – indeed, a majority of Americans in uniform during World War I never left the United States – and could shop in local stores in their off-duty hours. Frontline troops had ready access to postcards too – and not just while on leave. "Picture postcard shops were everywhere in the villages just behind the lines," wrote Tonie and Valmai Holt.[76] Sometimes these enterprises could be dangerously close to the fighting. American journalist Heywood Broun (1888-1939) visited Reims while the city was under German shelling, and despite the danger and destruction he noted, "a man who keeps a picture postcard shop in a building next door to the newspaper office." Broun noted that the proprietor remained open despite the fact that "his roof has been knocked down about his head and his business is hardly thriving."[77]

In shopping for postcards, soldiers had a wide variety from which to choose. They might pick up the same kinds of propaganda and patriotic cards as civilians. Like any peacetime tourist, the soldiers snapped up the usual tourist postcards with local scenes and landmarks. American troops – the vast majority of whom had never been outside the United States before – seemed particularly eager tourists. Pat Crowe saw postcards with "the usual views showing 'L'Eglise' [or] 'Place-de-something or other.' In this section there is always an 'Avenue Gambetta' and a 'Rue Victor Hugo.' The whole set of a dozen comes for two francs – one franc before the American occupation."[78] "At every town where the train stopped," claimed the historian of the U.S. Army's Base Hospital No. 18, "the commissary in the station was immediately mobbed and the boys toted off all they could find that was edible and all the post card views of the surrounding country."[79] Katharine Morris, a soldier welfare volunteer in France, "encountered two boys who told me how they had 'done' Paris." She quoted the soldiers as telling her the following:

---

[76] Holt and Holt, *Till the Boys Come Home*, 30.

[77] Heywood Broun, *The A.E.F.: With General Pershing and the American Forces* (New York: D. Appleton, 1918), 133.

[78] Crowe, *Aviator*, 57

[79] *History of Base Hospital No. 18, American Expeditionary Forces (Johns Hopkins Unit)* (Baltimore: Base Hospital 18 Association, 1919), 68.

Introduction

> "We stopped at a store and bought a bunch of post cards, all the famous buildings and everything. Then we got a taxi. After that all we'd do was to show the chauffeur a post card and he'd drive us to it, – then we'd show him another one, and so we kept a-goin' until we'd seen most all of Paris."[80]

Tourist cards could give the family back home a sense of the sights their soldier boys were seeing. "Sent Ruth and Alta some postal card pictures of the town," Albert Funkhouser wrote his parents. "If they arrive you can get some idea of a typical small French village."[81]

Photographers working around training camps and other installations peddled real photo postcards. Armed with postcard cameras, photographers could capture the images of the recruits, and then print up small batches of postcards they could then send home. Newly minted troops were anxious to be photographed and have their images printed onto postcard stock. Writing about the British Tommy, Tonie and Valmai Holt noted that "whole families would enlist and send their group picture back to the parents at home," and "individuals would proudly pose in their new uniform vaunting their newly formed identity. Often the uniform would be their finest suit of clothes."[82] For some, it was the first time they had had their photographs taken. It was the same at U.S. training camps. Among the first questions an American recruit had upon their arrival, according to William McCarthy of the 309th Field Artillery, were "when will I get my uniform, and when can I get my picture taken?"[83] Soldiers posed individually or in groups, on post or at off-post local studios with large flags or military background motifs. Once overseas, doughboys sometimes found that villagers behind the lines made a little extra money taking photographs and selling real picture postcards to the troops. All one needed was a postcard camera, some ink, and some card stock to go into business. While in the Alsatian village of Saulxures, Evan Alexander Edwards, the chaplain of the U.S. Army's 140th Infantry Regiment, billeted with a family "who had a bicycle shop, and made post-card photographs of many of the

---

[80] Katharine Duncan Morse, *Uncensored Letters of a Canteen Girl* (New York: H. Holt, 1920), 220.

[81] *In memoriam, Albert Craig Funkhouser, Co. F., 144 Inf., 36th Division, Paul Taylor Funkhouser, Co. B., 7th Machine Gun Bn., 3rd Division* (Evansville, IN: privately published, 1919), 32.

[82] Holt and Holt, *Till the Boys Come Home*, 30 and 70.

[83] William E. McCarthy, *Memories of the 309th Field Artillery* (Rochester, NT: Henry Conolly, 1920), 22.

men."[84] Many French and Belgian locals made cards specifically for Anglophone troops, and their captions often contained misspellings and grammatical errors. Indeed, the veracity of the captions is often open to question.

Beyond the ordinary cardboard postcards, French and Belgian merchants also sold a variety of colorful, hand-made cards embroidered with silk or lace. Some even came with small handkerchiefs enclosed, providing the recipient with not just a greeting but also a gift. "Silk cards could be bought with patriotic messages, flags of the allies, or regimental crests embroidered into them," wrote John Willoughby.[85] As in the pre-war years, silk cards could also be used to send birthday or holiday greetings. "There are post cards for all the fête days," wrote Pat Crowe, "done in China silk and lace paper, with 'Bon Noel' and 'Bonne Annee' or other touching inscription embroidered."[86] Some cards had the words "souvenir de France" or "souvenir de Belgique."

Postcards could also capture the emotions of the men on the front lines. Soldiers far from home and facing death used humor to cope with their fears. Many postcards marketed to British troops featured the popular cartoon character Old Bill. A grizzled older Tommy with a bushy moustache and an ornery disposition, Old Bill was the creation of a wounded British officer named Bruce Bairnsfather (1887-1959). One popular cartoon-turned-postcard featured Old Bill and another soldier in a shell hole while bullets and artillery shells flew overhead, his comrade looking frightened. "Well if you knows of a better 'ole," Old Bill tells him, "go to it."[87] Many postcards were highly sentimental. Young men in uniform, even the most educated and articulate, often had difficulties sorting through the maelstrom of emotions they felt at the front, be it fear, homesickness, romantic feelings for their wives or girlfriends, or the deep affection for their parents or siblings. Like modern-day greeting cards, postcard images often captured the emotional sentiment the soldiers felt but could not otherwise express. Embroidered silk cards were especially popular for this purpose. "Typical of the legends" on silk cards, wrote John Willoughby,

---

[84] Evan Alexander Edwards, *From Doniphan to Verdun: The Official History of the 140th Infantry Regiment* (Lawrence, KS: The World Company, 1920), 48

[85] Willoughby, *A History of Postcards*, 117.

[86] Crowe, *Aviator*, 57.

[87] Old Bill postcards came in sets of six cards entitled "Fragments from France," and were also published in book form, including in the United States. See Bruce Bairnsfather, *Fragments of France* (New York: G.P. Putnam, 1917) and *More Fragments from France* (New York: G.P. Putnam, 1918).

Introduction   xxix

"are 'To My Dearest Mother,' 'Forget Me Not,' 'Thinking of You Always,' and 'Home Sweet Home.'"[88] "By choosing the image," claimed de Vries, "the sender could perhaps convey feelings or sentiments more easily than by putting them into words."[89]

Postcards also satisfied the more prurient interests of young men. Erotic cards could "range from the very innocent," wrote de Vries, "through unabashedly erotic to the clearly pornographic."[90] These items were obviously not intended for correspondence – they would never have gotten past censors anyway – but rather were pinned up on the walls of dugouts or kept among a soldier's private possessions. France was by far the most important producer of such works, though soldiers of all countries consumed them. Americans had a particular reputation in Europe for their priggish views about sex, and in their writings many doughboys expressed their disapproval of such works. Arthur Joel of the 79th Division remembered that while on the march from the docks of Brest that local women approached the incoming troops selling wine, cognac, and "detestable post-card views." For Joel, it represented the "first indications of war-time immorality."[91] Pat Crowe declared such postcards "awful" and complained that "the worst of it is that they are displayed prominently in the show windows."[92] Fred Witt of the 135th Field Artillery remembered a "cluster of peasant stands outside the gate" of his artillery training camp near Bordeaux, where locals peddled a variety of items to the Americans. "In the name of art were proffered post-card views that would have shocked the Ohio Board of Censors out of business," he wrote, and claimed that although local merchants sold goods to the doughboys at inflated prices, such postcards were "the cheapest thing in France."[93]

Soldiers also purchased postcards with photographs of scenes from the front lines, which Guus de Vries labeled "reality" postcards. "Cards of this type are almost infinite in number and variety," he wrote. "They can show scenes from combat, destroyed homes, devastated villages, or towns, prisoners of war, wounded or dead soldiers, displaced civilians, military equipment, scenes from soldiers' daily lives and portraits or group photos,

---

[88] Willoughby, *A History of Postcards*, 117.

[89] de Vries, *The Great War through Picture Postcards*, 11.

[90] Ibid., 40.

[91] Arthur H. Joel, *Under the Lorraine Cross* (Charlotte, MI: The Charlotte Tribune, 1921), 14.

[92] Crowe, *Aviator*, 57.

[93] Fred Ralph Witt, *Riding to War with "A": A History of Battery A of the 135th Field Artillery* (Cleveland, C. Hauser, 1919), 85.

to name just a few."⁹⁴ Like official government photos or the postcards of *Daily Mail* or *Chicago Daily News*, reality postcards captured the sights of the front. However, reality postcards differed in some respects. They were typically real photo postcards, produced locally, and portrayed the war in a more frank and raw manner. Photographs of the deceased, for example, are far more gruesome than any images a censor would allow through the mail, and sometimes accompanied by snide commentary demeaning the enemy dead, suggesting they were intended as personal souvenirs rather than to be mailed. According to Tonie and Valmai Holt, postcard makers in "neutral states, like Holland, were able to obtain pictures of battle casualties and enterprising local publishers would produce cards for home consumption." Such postcards were extremely rare, they note, and claimed that they "never circulated freely in the combatant countries."⁹⁵ The photographer and manufacturer of these reality cards are usually unidentified, making it nearly impossible to ascertain their provenance. Indeed, many such cards were simply reproductions of press or official government photographs, made by entrepreneurs behind the lines.

Soldiers were also photographers themselves. The democratization of photography in the prewar years meant that many World War I soldiers went to war with personal cameras in their possession. Some recruits brought cameras to training camp. "I have had my picture taken about a hundred times," claimed Kenneth Gow while at Camp Wadsworth, South Carolina. "Every man that has a camera has come to me and asked if I wouldn't let him take my picture."⁹⁶ At the front, policies about cameras varied from army to army. British officials strongly discouraged soldier photography in the name of security, though not all obeyed such admonitions. Rules about cameras were less strict in the French and German armies. During the First World War, the U.S. military followed the British practice. However, during the various American military entanglements with revolutionary Mexico immediately preceding U.S. entry into the Great War, it was different. During operations like the 1914 occupation of Veracruz and the so-called "punitive" expedition of 1916-1917 to capture

---

⁹⁴ de Vries, *The Great War through Picture Postcards*, 27.
⁹⁵ Hot and Holt, *Till the Boys Come Home*, 68.
⁹⁶ Kenneth Gow, *Letters of a Soldier* (New York: H.B. Covert, 1920), 164.

the anti-American revolutionary Pancho Villa (1878-1923), American troops often had a camera in hand and sent home countless images.[97]

For the troops, producing photographic prints and real photo postcards took little effort. Like civilian producers behind the lines, men at the front only needed a camera, film, ink, and paper stock. As a volunteer ambulance driver with the American Field Service – a volunteer organization of Americans working on the Allied side of the lines – Julien Bryan (later a noted photographer and filmmaker) reached the front in 1916 before the United States had entered the war, and documented his activities in France with "a post-card sized camera." In making prints, Bryan and a comrade used "the loft of a barn for a laboratory," and remembered that "sometimes we printed by sunlight and sometimes we printed by means of the carbide headlights on one of the cars." Writing in 1918 after his return to America, Bryan offered some photographic tips for his countrymen headed to France. "I would advise anyone going over with the intention of taking pictures not to get a smaller camera, for although the larger size is occasionally troublesome, little pictures are always unsatisfactory." However, Bryan conceded that "this advice may be unnecessary," because "our authorities, like the British, are very strict about the use of cameras within the war zone."[98] Countless soldiers and sailors became amateur photographers. Some of the men even made a business out of selling their photos to private vendors, who then sold the postcards in local shops.[99]

During the First World War, the availability of photography tremendously altered the experience of the war and its perception.[100] Great War soldiers took countless snapshots to capture and memorialize their experiences. Indeed, soldier photography might well be considered its own sub-genre of the photographic craft. Frontline photography, as Brocks has noted, provides a more direct and personal representation of the war.[101] As Thomas Flemming and Ulf Heinrich put it, soldier photos are "living evidence for the pictorial perception of the World War."[102] However, soldier

---

[97] Paul J. Vanderwood, "The Picture Postcard as Historical Evidence: Veracruz, 1914," *The Americas* 45, 2 (1988): 202. Some of these Pancho Villa postcards are part of the Williwood Meador Collection: Pancho Villa and the Border Revolution at Porter Henderson Library, Angelo State University, San Angelo TX.

[98] Julien H. Bryan, *Ambulance 464* (New York: Macmillan, 1918), ix

[99] Brocks, *Die bunte Welt*, 238.

[100] For a detailed analysis of photography in war, see Bernd Hüppauf, *Fotografie im Krieg* (Paderborn: Wilhelm Fink, 2015).

[101] Brocks, *Die bunte Welt*, 238.

[102] Flemming and Heinrich, *Grüße aus dem Schützengraben*, 22.

snapshots offered highly selective images of war. Through the selection (or omission) of subject matter in their images, the soldier-photographers sought to frame perceptions of military life. As historian Paul J. Vanderwood observed in his study of U.S. troops in Mexico, soldier photography expresses "the way in which common combatants hoped to remember the event, and how they wanted others to view it."[103]

Photographic images, according to Bob Rogers, can be "usefully, but not rigidly, divided into three basic categories: directorial, improvisational and autophotographic images." Directorial photos, according to Rogers, are essentially staged scenes involving the "use of arranged or specially selected objects for the presentation of a personal point of view." Improvisational images, he writes, are "spontaneously created" photos in which subjects pose and interact with the photographer, "transforming an ordinary occurrence into a ritual recreation of the photographer's universe – a reaffirmation of the lives of the participants." Casual snapshots, claims Rogers, are "the purest form of improvisational photography." Autophotographic photos are more documentary in nature than improvisational ones, and require little if any photographer-subject interaction.[104]

Soldier-generated photographs and real photo postcards exhibit characteristics of each of Rogers' helpful classifications. Autophotographic images of war's destruction were common. There were countless photos of destroyed buildings and bridges, denuded and burned forests, fields full of shell holes and broken barbed wire, and other such scenes of destruction – not to mention pictures of tanks, guns, artillery pieces, and other implements of war. Such images highlighted both the sensationalism of war and fear the soldiers experienced. However, such scenes are usually portrayed in circumscribed ways. Soldier-photographers often obscured the link between their actions and destruction in the photographs. As Brocks noted, the causal relationship between the weaponry and its effects was rarely demonstrated in any one image. The weapons were decoupled from their effects on the soldiers, landscapes, and buildings that they destroyed; some famous examples are the Cathedral in Reims and the Library of Leuven. Violence and its consequences were often omitted from soldier photograph collections altogether.[105] Death, despite being an absolute certainty and reality of war, was excluded from the scenes.[106] Images of the dead and dismembered splayed across the rugged landscape of "no man's

---

[103] Vanderwood, "The Picture Postcard," 201.
[104] Rogers, "Photography and the Photographic Image," 30.
[105] Brocks, *Die bunte Welt*, 243-245.
[106] Ibid., 238-239.

land," were rarely displayed on most photographic picture postcards.[107] As Brocks observed, the glorification of violence, which comprised the later aesthetics of Fascism and National Socialism, was not yet dominant during the First World War; it was only in the war's final months — and to a limited audience — that such aesthetic changes were visible.[108]

More often, soldier snapshots and real photo postcards showed soldiers in harmonic group settings, as well as portraits of individuals. Bonds between fighting men are often strong and intimate. Indeed, camaraderie among soldiers often serves as a substitute for family bonds strained or severed during wartime. Soldiers often refer to their comrades as "brothers," for example, perhaps best expressed by Shakespeare's "band of brothers" speech in *Henry V*:

> We few, we happy few, we band of brothers;
> For he to-day that sheds his blood with me
> Shall be my brother; be he ne'er so vile

Soldier photography was a way to express and memorialize that brotherhood, find something redeeming in the otherwise horrific practice of war, and (to paraphrase Rogers) reaffirm the lives of those in the images. It is, therefore, no surprise that directorial and improvisational images of soldiers, sometimes posing next to static scenes of buildings, landscapes, or weapons, were a dominant motif in Great War soldier photography. The lack of combat in the images reflects the security and control the soldiers strove to depict. The war had destroyed the world they once knew, and as Christine Brocks suggests, the omission of violence in the photographs and on picture postcards recreated a non-violent hideaway for the consciousness of those plagued by war and destruction in their daily lives.[109] Human beings remained the focal point of postcards from the wartime era, even if the individuals in question were irrelevant to the war itself — a war that knew no heroes, but only blood, flesh, and bones, all destroyed by modern machines. The proliferated images suggested that men were still able to make a difference in war, while the reality was often that they would die in "no man's land" without any remembrance of their existence. The war's realities caused the soldiers to wish for an alternative world, and this world was often created on the back of a postcard.

Thus, the purpose of the picture postcards created by the combatants was not so much to depict the reality of war accurately, but rather to rede-

---

[107] Flemming and Heinrich, *Grüße aus dem Schützengraben*, 22.
[108] Brocks, *Die bunte Welt*, 239.
[109] Ibid., 18.

fine it. Those in the trenches wanted to remember their comrades, but not dwell on painful memories of death and dismemberment. The photographs of the soldiers were often transformed into postcards and sent home, where families could focus on values like camaraderie, and not on war's atrocities.[110] The soldiers thereby kept the reality of the war a secret. Because the war's violence was never openly communicated, the suffering of the soldiers, namely their fear and dread of battle, also could have led to the staged military displays in most of the photographs.

What did World War I soldiers do with their photograph and postcard collections? Just like peacetime civilian collectors, thousands gathered their images into scrapbooks or albums. Many scrapbooks were multimedia affairs, combining many different kinds of souvenir materials. Equating souvenir collecting to a disease, Pat Crowe noted that:

> In its more advanced stages, this unfortunate obsession takes the form known as Memory Books. This is a bulbous growth of the diary, due to the accumulation of various foreign objects, such as the small coins of all nations, kodak pictures of ruins with an American prominent in the foreground, French programs, menu cards from the transport Baltic, and colored clippings of pictures of aeroplanes.[111]

Being on the move, it was often difficult for military personnel to put together souvenir booklets during the war. However, families back home often kept scrapbooks documenting the military exploits of their loved ones, filled with items their soldier boy had sent home. Kenneth Gow sent his family several items he requested that his family keep for him. "Enclosed are one or two more orders affecting me which I should like inserted in my scrap-book," he wrote from Camp Wadsworth, South Carolina. From France he sent home several newspaper clippings, one a portrayal of American troops from a British newspaper. "Paste the enclosed clipping in my scrapbook," he wrote his family ten days before his death at the front in September 1918.[112]

How many World War I soldiers sent postcards through the mail, collected them, or put them in scrapbooks can never be known with certainty, though the number is undoubtedly in the millions. Given that the war came at the height of the global postcard craze, and that these small rectangular pieces of cardboard had so many wartime uses, it could hardly

---

[110] Flemming and Heinrich, *Grüße aus dem Schützengraben*, 19.

[111] Crowe, *Aviator*, 58.

[112] Gow, *Letters of A Soldier*, 274 and 376.

have been otherwise. Whether for communication, remembrance, a badge of their status as a war veteran, escapism, or simply because they liked a particular image, postcard collecting was a common pastime for those in uniform during the Great War, and among the countless soldiers returning from that "war to end all wars" with postcards in his possessions was a doughboy from Pennsylvania named Frank Marhefka.

Chapter 1

The World of Frank Marhefka

Frank Leonard Marhefka was born in Shamokin, Pennsylvania on 25 August 1888. In many ways, he was typical of the 4.5 million Americans who served in the U.S. armed forces during the First World War. A working class man from a small industrial town, Marhefka was conscripted into the army. He did not see combat. So far as is known, he left behind no letters, diaries, or other written accounts of his experiences in the Great War. There is only his postcard album. Who was this man who left behind an enigmatic collection of postcards?

Formative Years

Shamokin, Pennsylvania is located in Northumberland County, in the heart of anthracite coal country. Commercial mining in Shamokin dated to the 1820s, and the city and neighboring Coal Township grew up hand in hand with the expansion of American industrial production in the nineteenth century. Shamokin was a city of many different nationalities, with a pronounced ethnic pecking order. Its earliest settlers, English, Scottish, and German, formed the city's elite. Miners from Wales also brought valuable expertise to the Northumberland County coalfields. During the mid-nineteenth century, poor Irish immigrants did the dirtiest and most dangerous mining jobs, often working ten hours a day six days a week for very low wages. Children were a common sight in the mines. "Breaker boys" as young as eight were put to work removing slate and other impurities from the coal. Such exploitative conditions fed labor unrest. Northumberland County was a hotbed of the Molly Maguires, a secretive radical Irish workers' society noted for violent attacks on the powerful. A series of high profile arrests, trials, and executions in the 1870s quelled the movement.[1] As immigration patterns shifted in the late nineteenth century, Shamokin's population grew more diverse. Immigrants from southern Italy arrived in

---

[1] For more on the Molly Maguires, see Kevin Kenny, *Making Sense of the Molly Maguires* (New York: Oxford University Press, 1998).

the mines, but Eastern Europeans – Lithuanian, Ukrainian, and Polish – contributed the most to the city's labor force and growing population. Derisively called "Hunkies," Eastern Europeans occupied the bottom rung on Shamokin's social ladder by 1900. In addition to mining, Shamokin was also noted for silk manufacturing. Eagle Silk Company, founded there in 1903, employed the wives and daughters of many miners.[2]

Like many in Shamokin, Frank Marhefka was the son of immigrants.[3] His father, Antoni Marchewka, was born in Poland in 1849 and came to the Pennsylvania coalfields in the early 1880s with his wife Jozefa and their brood of young children. Antoni worked in the mines for nearly two decades, but by 1901 he had left the mines, Americanized his name to Anthony Marhefka, and opened a grocery store at the family's home at 429 South Vine Street in Shamokin.[4] Several of Anthony Marhefka's sons worked in the mines, but others took a different path. His son Anthony played professional baseball with several minor league teams across the Northeast, from Wilkes-Barre, Pennsylvania to New London, Connecticut. Another son, Joseph, became a shoe salesman. Frank also followed a retail path. Growing up, he likely worked in the family grocery store, then as a young man went into business with his brother Joseph. The 1913 Shamokin city directory lists Joseph and Frank as the proprietors of Marhefka Brothers, a shoe store located at 407 North Shamokin Street.[5]

---

[2] For more on the history of Shamokin and Northumberland County, Herbert C. Bell and J.J. John, *History of Northumberland County, Pennsylvania* (Chicago: Brown, Runk & Co., 1891); Shamokin Centennial Committee, *Greater Shamokin Centennial, 1864-1964* (Shamokin, PA: Shamokin Centennial Committee, 1964); and Janet MacGaffey, *Coal Dust On Your Feet: The Rise, Decline, and Restoration of an Anthracite Mining Town* (Lewisburg, PA: Bucknell University Press, 2013).

[3] For more on Polish immigration to the United States, see John J. Bukowczyk, *A History of Polish Americans* (New Brunswick, NJ: Transaction Publishers, 2008).

[4] *Boyd's Shamokin and Sunbury Directory: Containing the Names of the Citizens, a Compendium of the Government, and of Public and Private Institutions, 1886-1888* (Pottsville, PA: W. Harry Boyd, 1886), 104; *Boyd's Directory of Shamokin: Containing the Names of the Citizens, Compendium of the Government and of Public and Private Institutions, 1901-1903* (Reading, PA: W.H. Boyd, 1901), 123. Home grocery stores, known as "neighborhood stores," were common in turn-of-the-century Shamokin. They typically catered to an ethnic clientele, and extended generous credit to hard-pressed immigrant families. Home taverns were also common. For more, see MacGuffey, *Coal Dust On Your Feet*, 30-34.

[5] *Boyd's Directory of Shamokin: Containing the Names of the Citizens, A Compendium of the Government and of Public and Private Institutions, 1913-1915* (Reading, PA: W.H. Boyd, 1913), 176.

When World War I broke out in the summer of 1914, Shamokin and Coal Township seemed far from the horrors of the European battlefields. By 1914 the area's population had grown to 45,000. There were ten coal mines operating in the area, employing 12,000 people. The Eagle Silk Mill in Shamokin employed another 3,000. Indeed, the war seemed to stimulate the Northumberland County economy. *Greater Shamokin Centennial*, a historical pamphlet of the city prepared for the 100th anniversary of its incorporation, painted a rosy picture of the city in the years immediately before American entry into the war. "The area's mines ... were operating at full blast," noted its author, "producing coal with ever-increasing efficiency for an ever-widening market," and the city's factories were "turning out fabrics for use throughout the nation as well as abroad."[6] The bustling town boasted twenty hotels, twenty-seven churches (including St. Stanislaus Roman Catholic Church, which the Marhefka's attended), and five banks. Shamokin worked hard, but its citizens found leisure time too. Residents "took pride and pleasure in organizing and supporting bands and baseball teams, dances and minstrel shows, parades and picnics," claimed *Greater Shamokin Centennial*. Downtown Shamokin boasted five theaters and a variety of restaurants. "Independence Street, on Sunday evenings, was crowded with young promenaders," wrote the author, and "Johnny Moore's Ice Cream Parlor, situated in the triangle building at Independence and Orange Streets, was a popular meeting place at the time."[7] Frank Marhefka might well have been one of the young Shamokinites strolling along Independence Street and frequenting the ice cream parlor, but during these years he also experienced disappointments. His father died in 1915, and the Marhefka Brothers shoe store went out of business. By 1917, Frank was working as a salesman at the Isaac Dluge Clothing Store in Shamokin.

Upon entering the Great War in 1917, the United States found itself woefully unprepared. Its army stood at a mere 120,000 soldiers, with another 80,000 poorly trained members of the National Guard. Getting young men in uniform was one of the country's top priorities. Volunteer enlistments did not come close to meeting manpower needs, and in May 1917 President Woodrow Wilson signed the Selective Service Act authorizing conscription.[8] Under the law, local draft boards – 4,648 of them in all – were to register men in their communities between the ages of 21 and 31 (later

---

[6] *Greater Shamokin Centennial*, 51.

[7] *Greater Shamokin Centennial*, 54.

[8] For more on military conscription in the United States during World War I, see John Whiteclay Chambers II, *To Raise an Army: The Draft Comes to Modern America* (New York: Free Press, 1987).

expanded from 18 to 45), classify them, and then decide who would enter the service, keeping local economic needs in mind. Non-citizen immigrants could not be compelled to serve, though naturalized citizens and those who declared their intention to become citizens were subject to the draft. The first registration occurred on June 5, and among the young men signing up in Shamokin that day was 28-year-old Frank Leonard Marhefka. According to his draft registration card, Marhefka was of medium build with blond hair and grey eyes.[9]

Marhefka's local draft board did not pick him in its first round of selections, but hundreds of his neighbors were called up, and they departed Northumberland County to great fanfare. The nearby town of Mount Carmel staged a parade on 4 September which the local newspaper described as "one of the most unique and spectacular celebrations ever held in this section of the State." Communities from across coal country sent delegations to participate. Veterans of the Civil War and Spanish-American War marched, as did local elected officials, fraternal societies, the Boy Scouts, and students and faculty from public and parochial schools. Church, school, and local civic bands provided the music, among them "the superb Shamokin band." Worker organizations also marched, including a contingent from the United Mine Workers, and ethnic societies were well represented. "There was "the Bersaglieri Society, wearing the beautiful uniform and plume of our brave allies now battling against the Austrian hordes, with them came the Reggia Maria Society, the St. Luke's Slavish Society, and the St. Martin societies," as well as "the sons of Poland, band and society ... a big bunch of them." All of these ethnic participants, the paper claimed, were "splendid Americans." The main feature of the parade was, of course, the draftees themselves. "For many of them it was the very first marching they had ever done. They couldn't keep step, or distance, and their stride was unmilitary, but you could see by the way they held up their heads that they will measure up fully to the great task that has been entrusted to them."[10] On 19 September ninety-nine draftees left the train station at Shamokin, joining scores more from Mount Carmel, Kulpmont, Sunbury, and other neighboring communities, bound for Camp Meade, Maryland.[11]

---

[9] Draft registration card of Frank Leonard Marhefka, World War I Selective Service System Draft Registration Cards (National Archives Microfilm Publication M1509), Records of the Selective Service System (Record Group 163), National Archives, Washington, D.C.

[10] *Mount Carmel Item*, September 5, 1917.

[11] *Mount Carmel Item*, September 17, and September 19, 1917.

Judging by local newspaper accounts, Shamokin and surrounding communities got behind the war effort. Civic leaders raised money for service organizations like the American Red Cross and the Young Men's Christian Association (YMCA), and campaigned to sell government bonds. There was even an effort to send tobacco to local men in the service. "Suppose you were in France and just 'dying' for a cigarette or a pipe full," argued one newspaper article soliciting donations for the tobacco fund, "and suppose you had the price and could not get the smoke; then you would surely believe Sherman."[12] Ethnic Shamokinites were often eager to participate in the war effort, not just to prove their loyalty to their adopted country, but also to help their homelands gain independence.[13] Noncitizen immigrants often joined the U.S. military voluntarily. Hoping to capitalize on anti-German and anti-Austrian sentiment among Slavic immigrants in North America, France organized armies of Polish and Czechoslovakians and sent recruiters to the United States and Canada, many of whom came to Northumberland County. "Already several thousand men are [in] camp," one Polish recruiter told the *Mount Carmel Item*, "and every day hundreds are being enrolled in larger cities, as Chicago, Pittsburgh, New York, etc." A recruiter among the Czechs and Slovaks urged his ethnic compatriots to join the "fight against the Teutonic Powers."[14]

For the first year of American involvement in war, the Shamokin draft board did not see fit to call Marhefka into the army, though dramatic events of late 1917 and 1918 changed that. In November 1917, the communists overthrew the Russian government and effectively pulled that country out of the war, allowing Germany to focus its efforts on the Western Front. In March 1918, Germany began a series of offensives across the Western Front. The Allied cause looked bleak, and pressure grew to get American soldiers into battle as soon as possible. As events heated up on the Western Front, draft calls in the United States increased. Workers in industries essential to the war effort – like coal mining – often received draft exemptions. Though Marhefka managed to avoid the hard and dan-

---

[12] *Mount Carmel Item*, September 22, 1917. During the Civil War, General William Tecumseh Sherman (1820-1891) once famously said that "war is hell."

[13] For more on ethnic Americans in the U.S. military during the First World War, see Nancy Gentile Ford, *Americans All! Foreign-born Soldiers in World War* I (College Station: Texas A&M University Press, 2001).

[14] *Mount Carmel Item*, October 25, 1917, and November 17, 1917. For more on French recruitment of Slavic immigrants in the United States, see Joseph T. Hapak, "Selective Service and Polish Army Recruitment during World War I," *Journal of American Ethnic History* 10, 4 (1991): 38-61.

gerous work in the mines, his job as a salesman in a clothing store was not vital to the war effort, making him vulnerable to conscription, and in the spring of 1918 his number finally came up. By late spring, American forces appeared on the Western Front in growing numbers. On 27 May the U.S. First Division launched an attack on German troops holding the village of Cantigny in the Picardy region of France – the first American offensive of the war. It was a small operation, but the fight at Cantigny dominated newspaper headlines in Northumberland County and across the nation as Marhefka said his goodbyes to family and friends and prepared to enter the army. On 31 May 1918, Marhefka was sworn into service in Shamokin, and was one of more than one hundred men from Northumberland County to leave home that day and head off to war.[15]

The War Experience

The U.S. Army assigned Marhefka not to a fighting unit, but to the Quartermaster Corps. He began his army career at Camp Joseph E. Johnston near Jacksonville, Florida. Camp Johnston was founded in September 1917 to "centralize the newly commissioned and enlisted personnel of the Quartermaster Corps in order that the many and various organizations composing it could be uniformly disciplined, trained, and equipped." Enlisted men arriving at Camp Johnston received two weeks of basic military training, and were then assigned to one of the camp's numerous specialty schools. "Among the more common Quartermaster units organized at this camp," according to one report

> were supply companies, butchery companies, salvage units, graves registration units, clothing and bath units, typist and stenographic units, railhead detachments, motor-truck trains, miscellaneous Quartermaster units, sales commissary units, and units consisting of mechanics, plumbers, painters, and electricians. Student officers were trained as specialists in contracts; water, rail, and motor transportation; money accounts; property accounts; general administration and company administration; supplies, subsistence, and clothing and equipage; construction and repair; motor truck; motor car; motorcycle; and personnel.

---

[15] *Mount Carmel Item*, May 24, 1918, and June 1, 1918.

When Marhefka arrived in the summer of 1918, Camp Johnston was buzzing with activity. By August, it was home to nearly 30,000 troops and by the war's end, 82,020 officers and men had passed through its gates.[16]

In assigning recruits to job specialties, the Quartermaster Corps tried to take into account the soldier's prewar occupations and experiences. Those who worked in the restaurant business frequently became cooks and bakers, for example, while those with chauffeur experience or mechanical skills were assigned to motor transportation units. Though Marhefka had worked as a salesman before the war, the army initially assigned him to the Field Remount Squadron No. 309, working with horses and mules. His assignment there did not last long, however. Desperate for non-commissioned officers, the army combed the ranks of the recruits for possible leaders, and Marhefka – at age 29, a little older than the typical recruit – was a perfect candidate. He attained rank of sergeant on 5 September 1918, and on 11 September was reassigned to the Headquarters Detachment of Motor Supply Train No. 426, where he became a supply sergeant – more in keeping with his retail background.[17]

Motor Supply Train No. 426, consisting of six motor truck companies as well as its headquarters detachment, departed Camp Johnston on 24 September and made its way by train to Hoboken, New Jersey, the army's main port of embarkation for troops headed to Europe. On 26 September – while Marhefka and his comrades were en route to Hoboken – the AEF launched the Meuse-Argonne Offensive, the largest U.S. military operation of the war. The attack was part of a larger Allied "Grand Offensive" to push the Germans out of France and Belgium. It was the hardest fighting the American troops had yet seen, and must surely have been the topic of considerable discussion as Motor Supply Train No. 426 arrived in New Jersey and prepared for departure. On 30 September the eight officers and 229 men of the 426th (minus Motor Truck Company No. 534, which made the voyage separately) departed the United States on the RMS *Caronia*, a

---

[16] Henry G. Sharpe, *The Quartermaster Corps in the Year 1917 in the World War* (New York: The Century Co., 1921), 403-411.

[17] Frank L. Marhefka file, World War I Veterans Service and Compensation File, Records of the Department of Military and Veterans Affairs (RG 19), Pennsylvania State Archives, Harrisburg, Pennsylvania.

British passenger liner converted into a troopship for the war. It arrived at Brest, France on 13 October 1918.[18]

Troops arriving at Brest marched from the docks to a camp at Pontanezen north of the city, to recuperate from their ocean voyage and prepare transportation inland to their assignment. Camp Pontanezen could be a miserable place. The cool, moist climate of Brittany chilled the arriving doughboys to the bone, even in summer. To make matters worse, the army was unprepared to handle the vast number of soldiers arriving each day. The result was mud and confusion. Ray Johnson of the 37th Division recalled his arrival one evening in June 1918:

> We marched three miles through the cold, heavy mist that was rolling in from the sea, and finally pitched pup-tents haphazard in a wet field, which had evidently been used for the same purpose before. This was the "Rest Camp" we had heard about where we were to rest and clean up for a few days! The morning sun revealed a chaos of confusion that the night had shrouded; pup-tents set at random, equipment scattered everywhere, and piles of rations and field kitchen impedimenta lying on the ground. Everything was cold and soaked with dew, but under the enlivening influence of the sun we set about the business of "straightening up" with a will, and by noon had produced an orderly, clean encampment.[19]

Conditions at Pontanezen attracted the attention of Congress and became a national scandal. Throughout 1918, the army worked feverishly to construct barracks, mess halls, roads, and wooden "duckboard" walkways to mitigate the problem of mud. Arriving troops at this "rest camp" often found themselves assigned to construction duties. By war's end, army engineers had constructed approximately 850 structures, though many transitory troops still stayed in tents.[20] Whether Marhefka and his comrades stayed in tents or barracks is not known, but it was undoubtedly cold and wet, and a cacophony of hammering and rumbling trucks filled their ears. On 18 October the 426th left Pontanezen and headed toward the front.

---

[18] Form No. 491 for Motor Supply Company No. 426, Records of Motor Supply Train No. 426, Records of Motor Supply Trains, Records of the American Expeditionary Forces (RG 120) (henceforth Records of Motor Supply Train No. 426), National Archives, College Park, Maryland.

[19] Ray Neil Johnson, *Heaven, Hell, or Hoboken* (Cleveland: O.S. Hubbell, 1919), 38.

Marhefka did not reach the fighting front, though he got close to it. The maintenance of vehicles in the AEF, as well as nearly all other support functions, came under the authority of the Services of Supply (SOS). From its headquarters at Tours on the Loire River, the SOS was in charge of more than 600,000 doughboys – roughly one third to total AEF strength. The SOS was responsible for American operations in nearly all areas behind the front. To manage such a vast area, the SOS divided its operations to three geographic regions. Base Sections, built around port cities such as Brest, Saint-Nazaire, and Bordeaux, took in supplies and prepared them for shipment inland. From there, the army transported goods to the Intermediate Section, which covered most of central and southern France. Here material was processed and stockpiled. Beyond that lay the Advance Section, just behind the front in northeastern France, where materiel was organized and sent off to the fighting units. The town of Neufchâteau, thirty miles behind the Saint-Mihiel Sector of the front lines on the upper reaches Meuse River, hosted Advance Section headquarters.

The main American line of communication through France ran from the Atlantic ports through the Loire Valley and into the Advance Section. The army transported most goods by rail, and prepared them for combat units at railroad "regulation stations" near the front. But as the tempo of the American buildup increased through 1918, railroad lines became clogged with traffic, so the army increasingly began to supplement rail transportation with motor vehicle convoys. It was the dawn of the automobile age, and motor transport had become so important that the army created the Motor Transport Corps (MTC) in July 1918, under the command of General M.L. Walker, as an entity separate from the Quartermaster Corps. The new MTC was responsible for the transportation of people and goods by vehicle, as well as the maintenance of nearly all vehicles – from three-ton trucks to bicycles. Only tanks and artillery tractors fell outside the purview of the MTC.[21]

Maintenance and repair of vehicles was a constant concern, whether due to accidents, combat damage, or general wear and tear. To maintain the fleet, the MTC established three kinds of repair facilities. Minor repairs

---

[20] United States War Department, *Historical Report of the Chief Engineer: Including All Operations of the Engineering Department, American Expeditionary Forces, 1917-1919* (Washington: GPO, 1919), 338-340.

[21] For more in the Motor Transport Corps in the First World War, see United States War Department, *Report of the Chief of the Motor Transport Corps* (Washington: GPO, 1920). For more on the history of logistics and the U.S. Army, see James A. Huston, *The Sinews of War: Army Logistics, 1775-1953* (Washington: Office of the Chief of Military History, United States Army, 1966).

were done at mobile service parks. More than half of the 102 MTC mobile service parks were attached to front line units; each combat division typically had three of them. Journalist Isaac Marcosson (1876-1961), who reported on SOS activities, described these units as "motor hospitals on wheels," and noted how they often "set up in a wheat-field or alongside an orchard with little French children as interested spectators."[22] The remainder of the service parks maintained vehicles behind the lines. Those vehicles in need of major repairs were brought to one of eight facilities called overhaul parks. These parks were usually located along railroad lines, about thirty miles behind the front on average, and capable of working on several hundred vehicles at a time. They also served as advance supply depots for the MTC. "Every piece of mechanical transport used by the American Expeditionary Force," Marcosson observed, "must be overhauled periodically. It is done at the Overhaul Park."[23] Irreparable vehicles were sent to a Reconstruction Park, where they were disassembled and parts salvaged for use on other vehicles. The MTC had only two such facilities, one at Verneuil near Nevers, and the other at Romorantin in the Loire Valley.[24]

Throughout its existence, the MTC was starved for personnel and materiel. With an authorized strength of 46,470 troops, at the time of the armistice the MTC had only 28,082.[25] Shipping enough trucks and spare parts across the Atlantic was a major problem for the army. "The AEF never did have half the vehicles called for in tables of organization," wrote historian James A. Huston.[26] "I believe that in motor transportation the United States has less to be proud of than any other one activity with which the S.O.S. was concerned," declared General Johnson Hagood (1873-1948), the SOS chief of staff. "With the streets of Washington jammed with army and civilian cars," he complained:

---

[22] Isaac F. Marcosson, *S.O.S. America's Miracle in France* (New York: John Lanes, 1919), 195.

[23] Ibid., 195-196.

[24] For more on vehicle repair operations, see Allied and Associated Powers (1914-1920), *Report of the Military Board of Allied Supply* (Washington: GPO, 1924-1925), vol. 2, 722-735; United States War Department, *Organization of the Services of Supply* (Washington: GPO, 1921), 62-68; United States Army, Center for Military History, *United States Army in the World War, 1917-1919* (Washington: U.S. Army Center for Military History, 1988), vol. 14, 158-159.

[25] *Report of the Military Board of Allied Supply*, vol. 2, 733-735; *Organization of the Services of Supply*, 62.

[26] Huston, *Sinews of War*, 369.

the 33rd Division on the British front did not have a single car that could be trusted to go twenty miles without a breakdown ... and the 66th Field Artillery Brigade had to manufacture its own spark plugs out of gas pipe, copper wire, and chewing gum. With traffic cops on every corner of the training camps at home and thousands of cars and trucks in reserve, we were put to the mortification of having to borrow transportation from the British and the French.[27]

Despite his complaints, Hagood took pains to compliment the soldiers of the MTC who did hard work under trying circumstances. "No one in France worked harder than the men who assembled, operated, and repaired the motor transportation," he wrote. "They ran their trucks at the front without lights at night over roads congested with traffic and cut up by shell holes. They kept them going without spare parts, material, or facilities for repair. They delivered the goods, but—!!"[28]

Marhefka and Motor Supply Train No. 426 were based at the overhaul park at Neufchâteau, not far from headquarters of the SOS Advance Section. The American military had transformed this small town of roughly 4,000 people and its environs into a major base of operations. The Advance Section headquarters and the MTC overhaul park were just some of many U.S. Army facilities in the area. There was a vast hospital complex in the neighboring village of Bazoilles, which according to war artist Jules A. Smith (1880-1949), "stretched into long train-like rows of wooden ward buildings which ended in lines of canvas tents, crossed the Meuse and the highway and sprouted again in more rows of tents and wooden buildings."[29] Surgery technician Frederick Pottle (1897-1987) also noted the cemetery adjacent to the hospital, where those who did not survive their wounds or illnesses were buried. "Each grave has a little green cross of wood with the man's identification tag nailed to it," he observed, "and an American flag."[30] Marhefka's duties likely took him to the railroad regulating station at Liffol-le-Grand, ten kilometers southwest of Neufchâteau. Completed in October 1918, the rail facility, according to one postwar report, consisted of "45 miles of track, a storage depot with 18 standard warehouses, engine terminal, bakery buildings, and accommodations for the shelter of 4,000 men, thus placing it among the more important of the

---

[27] Johnson Hagood, *The Services of Supply: A Memoir of the Great War* (Boston: Houghton Mifflin, 1927), 343.

[28] Ibid., 344.

[29] Jules A. Smith, *In France with the American Expeditionary Forces* (New York: A.H. Hahlo, 1919), 44.

[30] Frederick Pottle, *Stretchers* (New Haven: Yale University Press, 1929), 93

supply distribution centers created for the American Expeditionary Forces."[31] Among the Americans based at Neufchâteau during Marhefka's time there was a young Red Cross worker from Missouri named Walt Disney (1901-1966). When not serving doughnuts and coffee to soldiers passing through the area, Disney peddled cartoon caricatures and even fabricated battlefield souvenirs for soldiers in transit. According to one biographer, Disney and a friend got their hands on some German helmets, "scuffed them up with dirt, shot a hole in them and sold them as authentic war booty."[32]

Motor Supply Train No. 426 arrived in Neufchâteau on 21 October, and got right to work. Meuse-Argonne campaign had reached a crucial juncture. German forces proved tough to budge, but by mid-October their lines in the Meuse-Argonne region began to give way. As the Allies pushed the Germans back, vehicle maintenance became ever more important, as supply lines for advancing units grew longer. As a supply sergeant, Marhefka probably fought his war from behind a desk in Neufchâteau, and rarely if ever got near the front lines. The surviving records of Motor Supply Train No. 426 reveal little about the volume of work, and no letters or diaries of unit members are known to survive, but 426th must have done a lot of work and done it well during these crucial days. After the armistice, General Walker saw fit to recognize the 426th with a letter of commendation. "Since the arrival of this train in France until the present time, several companies of this train have done splendid work in varied activities, especially during the high pressure of the last months of 1918," he wrote. "Motor Supply Train #426 has a record of achievement of which all the officers and men may be justly proud, and which also reflects greatly to the credit of the Motor Transportation Corps."[33]

With the armistice of 11 November 1918, the Great War was over. Now the typical doughboy wanted nothing more than to go home, but the 426th stayed in place at Neufchâteau. Though their brief wartime service had been exemplary, disciplinary problems now cropped up among the men. Unit records from this period reported soldiers talking back to superiors or going absent without leave, as well as other lapses of military comportment. "It has come to the attention of the train commander," wrote the unit adjutant, "of the laxity in appearance of the men in this train." There

---

[31] *Historical Report of the Chief Engineer*, 314.

[32] Neal Gabler, *Walt Disney: The Triumph of American Imagination* (New York: Knopf, 2006), 40.

[33] Director, Motor Transportation Corps to C.O., Motor Supply Train #426, August 11, 1919, Records of Motor Supply Train No. 426.

were also problems with proper respect for rank. "Company commanders will arrange to have the sergeants in their organizations quartered separately from the enlisted men," the order continued, and also complained that "there is considerable familiarity between officers and enlisted men. This will stop at once."[34] The order must have had the desired effect, since it was rescinded less than a week later.[35] None of the documented disciplinary problems involved Marhefka.

In order to keep up morale, the army granted leave to soldiers liberally. On 1 April 1919, Marhefka applied for leave to visit the city of Menton on the French Riviera, a popular postwar leave center. In his application, Marhefka noted that he had "never had a leave."[36] The YMCA operated scores of leave centers for doughboys in France and Germany after the armistice, and with its sunnier climate and reputation for luxury, the French Riviera was perhaps the most popular destination of all. Leave trains streamed daily from rainy northern France down to the Riviera, loaded with doughboys anxious for some rest and relaxation. At one point, a thousand soldiers a day made the run from the U.S. Army regulating station at Is-sur-Tille to Menton. Boisterous troops on the leave trains frequently got into trouble. "The accident rate of troops travelling over our lines of communication had been high," noted one report:

> These accidents were for the most part clearly due to the carelessness of the men and the lack of discipline. During the warm weather the temptation was great for soldiers to get out of cars where they were crowded and to ride between or on top of the cars, or with their legs and heads hanging out the doors. The clearance between cars and bridges and tunnels in French railways is considerably less than clearances in the United States. In many instances it is only six inches. An active campaign was started by the Transportation Service, posters and warning notices … distributed among the troops at points of entrainment. Although these measures unquestionably helped the situation, they were never thoroughly effective because the commanding officers, in the majority of cases,

---

[34] Headquarters, Motor Supply Train #426, Special Order No. 12, March 2, 1919, Records of Motor Supply Train No. 426.

[35] Headquarters, Motor Supply Train #426, Special Order No. 13, March 8, 1919, Records of Motor Supply Train No. 426.

[36] Frank L. Marhefka to C.O., Motor Supply Train 426, 1 April 1919, Records of Motor Supply Train No. 426.

did not attempt to enforce restrictions laid down by the Transportation Service.[37]

Once the doughboys got to the Rivera, the unruly behavior often continued. Medical officers, for example, noted that prophylactic treatments for sexually transmitted infections in leave areas were "about nine times [higher than] that of the home sections," wrote one army physician, "thus indicating that venereal exposure was tremendously augmented by the men going on leave."[38] There were plenty of more wholesome recreational activities in the leave areas as well. According to the YMCA, the Riviera "afforded unexcelled opportunities for driving over the Corniche, climbing the olive covered hills, sailing the blue waters of the Mediterranean or flying planes along the coast." Like other tourists, the doughboys also picked up some souvenirs of their Rivera vacation, including postcards. Between 1 December 1918 and the closing of YMCA operations on 10 May 1919, the YMCA in Menton maintained 2,484 hotel rooms and processed more than 27,000 soldiers on leave.[39] Precisely what Marhefka did for entertainment there is not known. Indeed, it is not even clear that he actually made it to Menton before the closure of the YMCA facility.

In June 1919, Motor Supply Train No. 426 moved from Neufchâteau to Langres, and took up new duties. Located in the Haute Marne region of eastern France, Langres had a long military history. A hilltop city at the headwaters of the Marne, the military significance of Langres had been recognized since the days of the ancient Romans, who fortified it with a wall – portions of which still survive today. In the nineteenth century the French army constructed a huge citadel less than half a kilometer south of Langres, and filled the surrounding countryside with subsidiary forts, artillery batteries, and ammunition magazines to protect France from invasion from the east. During World War I, Langres became a beehive of American military activity. The U.S. Army transformed the city and the surrounding countryside into a vast education center, where the inexperienced Americans learned the arts of war. There were schools for chemical warfare, engineering, tactics, administration, medicine, and a host of other technical specialties – even one for pigeon handlers. The existence of the vast training complex was supposed to be secret, and referred to in

---

[37] *United States Army in the World War*, vol. 14, 241.

[38] George Walker, *Venereal Diseases in the American Expeditionary Forces* (Baltimore: Medical Standard Book Company, 1922), 20.

[39] Frederick Morgan Harris and William H. Taft, eds., *Service with Fighting Men: An Account of the American Young Men's Christian Associations in the World War* (New York: Association Press, 1922), 151 and 154.

official correspondence only by its army postal address, APO 714, though the complex was so large that one officer who trained there later wrote, "to believe that the Germans were ignorant of all this was severely to strain one's credulity."[40]

Included in the Langres training complex was a tank school, commanded by Captain George S. Patton, Jr. (1885-1945) – who would later gain fame as America's foremost armor commander – near the tiny village of Bourg, just south of Langres. After the armistice, Bourg also became the home of Motor Reception Park No. 714, to which Marhefka and Motor Supply Train No. 426 were assigned beginning 14 June 1919. With the war over, army vehicles were brought to collection points like the Bourg reception park, where they were then classified as to condition and sold off. One army inspection conducted shortly after Marhefka's arrival at Bourg found 23,812 "salable vehicles" at the Bourg reception park, including 6,412 motorcycles and 1,325 bicycles. Many vehicles arrived in badly damaged condition. "Experience has proven," wrote one army officer inspecting the Bourg facility in June 1919,

> That cars brought in in a badly wrecked condition have a much higher selling value when knocked down. Consequently, cars that would not be repairable are taken [apart], and all serviceable spare parts, motors, wheels, axles, etc., are carefully segregated according to class and type.... Material salvaged from wrecked cars that has no conceivable value as spare parts is placed in salvage heaps and sold as junk.

The inspector heaped praise on the 900 officers and men stationed at the facility. "This work is systematically done, and the appearance of the park, the lack of confusion, the system of classification as to serviceability and type of various vehicles," he wrote, was "satisfactory in every way," and that the "segregation and classification is done with intelligence and thoroughness."[41]

Marhefka and his unit's tenure at Bourg were brief. They departed on 23 August and three days later were back at Camp Pontanezen outside Brest awaiting shipment home. While awaiting transport, the soldiers were de-

---

[40] E. Alexander Powell, "A.P.O. 714: The University of the A.E.F.," *Scribner's Magazine* 65, 4 (1919): 414.

[41] United States Congress, House of Representatives, Select Committee on Expenditures in the War Department, *War Expenditures: Hearings Before Subcommittee No. 3 (Foreign Expenditures)*, Serial 4 – Parts 1-25, vol. 1 (Washington: GPO, 1920), 421-422.

loused and inspected while they waited impatiently. The camp was still a construction zone, with soldiers in transit once again drafted into labor details. Doughboy reviews of the facility varied. "Camp Pontanezen at this time was a marvel of cleanliness and efficiency," claimed army chaplain Gregory Mabry of the 54th Infantry Regiment.[42] Ray Johnson of the 37th Division, who passed through in June 1918, still found Pontanezen a "sea of mud," though he now noted that "the tents were floored with wood, and a network of duckboards provided foot paths." Johnson also enjoyed "motion-pictures" and "free cocoa and doughnuts" which welfare organizations provided.[43] "The three chief factors of life" at Pontanezen, claimed James Thayer Addison (1887-1953) of the First Gas Regiment, were "deep mud, hard labor, and wild rumors." Addison also noted that three members of his unit died on influenza there. "Their deaths, so long after the fighting was over and on the eve of our return to the rewards of home" he wrote, "brought especially deep regret."[44]

Motor Supply Train No. 426 sailed from Brest on 28 August and arrived at New York Harbor on 11 September, landing at the Bush Terminal in Brooklyn. The army officially disbanded Motor Supply Train No. 426 at Camp Dix, New Jersey on 17 September 1919. In all, Marhefka spent fourteen months in the U.S. Army, and not quite one year overseas, a time, he, however, documented with the following postcards and photographs.

---

[42] Gregory Mabry, *Recollections of a Recruit: The Official History of the U.S. Fifty-Fourth Infantry* (New York: Schilling, 1919), 138.

[43] *Johnson, Heaven, Hell, or Hoboken*, 174.

[44] James Thayer Addison, *The Story of the First Gas Regiment* (Boston: Houghton Mifflin, 1919), 197-198.

Chapter 2

Frank Marhefka's Postcard Collection

The Frank Marhefka postcard collection consists of 159 images of the First World War, glued onto paper sheets and bound into an album. Nearly all of the postcards fall into the category of "reality" postcards, as defined by Guus de Vries and explained in the Introduction. Given that Marhefka worked as a supply sergeant behind the lines, he would not likely have seen such scenes himself, although he may have made occasional forays into battle areas, or witnessed war-torn landscapes in his movements across France. Exactly where he acquired the postcards, or if he created some of them himself, is unknown. Neufchâteau and Langres, where he spent most of the war, were filled with doughboys, as well as local French civilians who might have manufactured and sold the images to him. Some may also have been acquired while on leave in Menton. It seems most likely that he purchased them after the armistice, when his workload would have diminished considerably. With his departure from France imminent in the summer of 1919, Marhefka would also have been motivated to purchase souvenirs before leaving. The gory nature of some of the postcards also suggests they were acquired after wartime censorship regulations had been relaxed. Several postcards depict scenes from the reception park at Bourg, indicating that they were produced sometime in the summer of 1919, and likely for the small group of soldiers stationed there.

Nearly all of the images in Marhefka's collection are not postcards in a technical sense at all, but rather real photographic copies of wartime postcards printed on postcard stock. Most measure about 4 ½" x 3 ½" (11cm x 8.5cm), and some are even as small as 3" x 2 1/4" (9cm x 5.5cm), whereas the typical postcard of the day measured 5 ½" x 3 ½" (14cm x 9cm). Many appear to be hand cut and vary slightly in size, suggesting local, small-scale production. Indeed, a few seem out of focus, suggesting quick and shoddy production. In none of the images is the photographer or manufacturer identified.

Most of the postcards seem to come from three distinct manufacturers, and Marhefka likely bought them in sets. One set, comprising the bulk of the collection, has captions written in English inside a white banner. They are most likely official French war photographs, acquired by a postcard maker. Their English captions suggest these cards were made specifically for Anglophone customers. Most are of battle scenes, though wartime leaders, ships, cemeteries, and other more generalized wartime images are also included. Most cards from this source are 4 ½" x 3 ½" (11cm x 8.5cm), though a few measure 3" x 2 1/4" (9cm x 5.5cm). The second group, also with English captions, are 3" x 2 1/4" (9cm x 5.5cm). These too are of front-line scenes, though often depict combat and its victims more graphically, and contain several images taken behind German lines. The final set of images are of Motor Reception Park No. 714 in Bourg, France, where Marhefka spend his last days in France. Some have captions written in French, but most appear to be standard photographic prints. Marhefka likely wrote the captions for these images himself on the album page beneath the photographs and it is conceivable that he might even have been the photographer.

Marhefka was hardly alone in returning to the United States with a collection of postcards. These and similar images can be found in museum and library collections across the United States. Several repositories have digitized these postcards and placed them online, including the National World War I Museum, the Tennessee in World War I collection that can be found and accessed through in the Tennessee Virtual Archive[1]; the Veterans History Project of the U.S. Library of Congress (www.loc.gov/vets), and the World Digital Library (www.wdl.org).

What follows is Marhefka's postcard collection. Each image appears in the order in which he arranged them in his album. Where appropriate, a brief historical sketch accompanies the images, providing historical context, commentary, and suggestions for further reading.

---

[1] teva.contentdm.oclc.org/cdm/landingpage/collection/WWI.

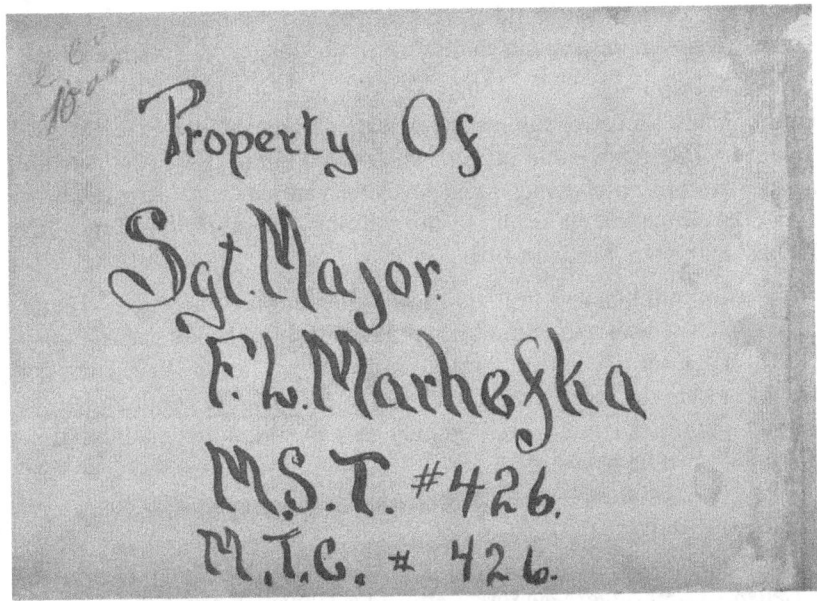

No.1: Marshall [sic] Foch & General Pershing at Chaumont, American G.H.Q.

Marshal Ferdinand Jean Marie Foch (1851-1929) was a French general who in March 1918 became the Commander-in-Chief of the Allied Armies.

At the end of the First World War, he advocated for a harsh peace treaty with Germany in the hope it would abolish the danger of another war.

General of the Armies John Joseph Pershing (1860-1948) served as the commanding officer of the American Expeditionary Force (AEF) in 1917 and 1918. Like many other officers who served in the Great War, Pershing advocated for frontal assaults and was later blamed for causing unnecessary U.S. casualties. He achieved the rank of General of the Armies (the highest in the U.S. Army) in 1919.

The two commanders are shown at a meeting at Chaumont (Haute-Marne) in Northeastern France, where Pershing established his headquarters to be closer to the front and to avoid the politics of Paris. Foch and Pershing were the most powerful leaders in the chain of command above Sergeant Marhefka, and he respectfully gave them the first position in his album of wartime postcards.

Further Readings:

Greenhalgh, Elizabeth. *Foch in Command: The Forging of a First World War General.* Cambridge/New York: Cambridge University Press, 2011.

Lacey, Jim. *Pershing.* New York: Palgrave Macmillan, 2008.

Woodward, David R.: *The American Army and the First World War.* New York: Cambridge University Press, 2014.

No. 2 and 3: French "75" in Abri; French Grenadiers (Marne)

When the First World War began, the French Army used around 4,000 75 mm field guns, the Canon de 75 modèle 1897, which had been produced since the late nineteenth century. It was usually referred to as "French 75," or simply the "75" and is still in use as a saluting gun of the French Army today. Its hydro-pneumatic recoil mechanism was responsible for the highest grade of stability during a firing sequence, which is why the gun did not have to be re-aimed after every shot. At a distance of about five miles, the "French 75" was able to deliver 15 shots per minute.

On the Western Front, soldiers often spent their days waiting for the next battle to begin. This photograph was taken in the Marne region of France, east of Paris. It was in the First Battle of the Marne, 6-10 September 1914, that Allied forces prevented the German Army from successfully fulfilling the ambitious goals of the Schlieffen Plan to envelop Paris in the opening stages of the war. Four years of bloody trench warfare followed. The Marne was the scene of still more bitter fighting during the German offensives of 1918 – this time involving American troops.

Further Readings:

Benoît, Christian. *Le canon de 75: Une gloire centenaire*. Vincennes: Service historique de l'Armée de terre, 1996.

Herwig, Holger. *The Marne, 1914: The Opening of World War I and the Battle that Changed the World*. New York: Random House, 2009.

No. 4: Clemenceau Visiting French Aviation Camp Near Front

Georges Clemenceau (1841-1929) served his second term as French Prime Minister from 1917 to 1920, and held this important political position during the last two years of World War I.

Further Readings:

Gottfried, Ted. *George Clemenceau*. New York: Chelsea House, 1987.

Watson, David Robin. *Georges Clemenceau: A Political Biography*. New York: David McKay Company, 1976.

No. 5 and 6: Big French Searchlight Combing the Sky for Planes; Night Flight at le Bourget

World War I saw the dawn of air power. When the war began, airplanes were used mainly for reconnaissance. As the war went on, "pursuit" planes emerged to destroy enemy observation planes and balloons, as well as attack ground troops. Still later, combatants used aircraft to bomb behind enemy lines in an effort to destroy factories and deflate civilian morale. With the rise of air power came air defenses, such as anti-aircraft guns. Searchlights, like the one seen here, spotted planes for the gunners during night raids.

Le Bourget airport is located in the northeastern suburbs of Paris, not far from today's Charles de Gaulle International Airport. This airfield is perhaps most famous for being the place where Charles Lindbergh completed the first solo transatlantic flight in 1927.

Further Readings:

Lee, Kennett. *The First Air War, 1914-1918*. New York: Free Press, 1991.

Martel, René. *L'Aviation française de bombardement (des origines au 11 novembre 1918)*. Paris: P. Hartmann, 1939. In English: *French Strategic and Tactical Bombardment Forces of World War I*. Lanham, MD: Scarecrow Press, 2007.

No. 7: Lake Longemer – Dinner at an American Camp

Lac de Longemer is a lake in Vosges, an eastern region of France, around 280 miles southeast of Paris. When the United States entered the war in 1917, there was very little fighting in the Vosges region. Newly-arrived American troops often spent time in such "quiet sectors" in order to acclimate themselves to life in the trenches and gain valuable combat experience.

No. 8 and 9: Machine Gun on Nieuport "Chasse" Plane; Abondoned [sic] German "Chasse" Plane

An "avion de chasse" is a fighter plane, then commonly known in the Anglophone world as pursuit plane. Nieuport was a French producer of planes, especially known for its Neuport 17 C.1, a sesquiplane fighter used by the French Air Force during the Great War.

Further Readings:

Bruce, J.M. *Nieuport Aircraft of World War One.* London: Arms and Armour Press, 1988.

Franks, Norman. *Nieuport Aces of World War 1.* Oxford: Osprey, 2000.

No. 10: Heavy German Guns Captured by English

Artillery played a major role during the First World War, especially since the new and heavy attrition warfare of the 20th century demanded steady supplies in bigger guns and higher amounts of shells. The image appears to show different kinds of German guns: a German 21cm mortar, a 77mm howitzer as well as an L 40 Artillery Gun.

Further Readings:

Strong, Paul and Sanders Marble. *Artillery in the Great War*. Barnsley: Pen & Sword, 2014.

Terraine, John. *White Heat: The New Warfare 1914-18*. London: Sidgwick & Jackson, 1982.

No. 11 and 12: Capt. Guynemer in Full Flight; Capt. Guynemer in "Old Charles"

Georges Guynemer (1894-1917) was a French pilot and the heroic fighter ace of France, counting 54 reported victories in aerial fights. "Vieux Charles" (Old Charles) was the name of his plane.

Guynemer was just one of several pilots who gained fame during the war. In contrast to the mud, blood, and impersonal mechanized slaughter of the trenches, the aerial "dogfights" between pilots seemed to suggest that bravery, romance, nobility, and individualism still had a place in war. Perhaps the most famous of all these "knights of the air" was Germany's "Red Baron," Manfred von Richthofen (1892-1918). By 1918, there were also quite a number of American pilots who fought in the aerial battles of the Great War.

Further Readings:

Binot, Jean-Marc. *Georges Guynemer*. Paris: Fayard, 2017.

Gibbons, Floyd. The Red Knight of Germany: The Story of Baron von Richthofen. San Francisco: Verdun Press, 2014.

Hudson, James J. *In Clouds of Glory: American Airmen Who Flew With the British During the Great War.* Fayetteville: University of Arkansas Press, 1990.

Hynes, Samuel. *The Unsubstantial Air: American Fliers in the First World War*. New York: Farrar, Straus, & Giroux, 2014.

No. 13: American Artillery Near Lenoncourt (Meuse)

Lenoncourt is a commune in the region of Grand Est — Département Meuse — in France, just east of Nancy. This image is remarkably similar to no. 23 below.

No. 14 and 15: The French "Chasse" Plane Ready for Flight; Caudron Plane

Given the novelty and romance of aerial operations at the time, pictures of aircraft appear frequently in wartime postcard sets. Marhefka may also have had a personal interest in aviation, and specifically sought out images like these.

The Société des Avions Caudron was one of France's aircraft manufacturers, founded in 1909 by the brothers Gaston (1882-1915) and René Caudron (1884-1959). While Gaston died in an aircraft accident in 1915, his brother continued the business until Nazi Germany occupied northern France in 1940. Famous models related to the Great War are the Caudron G.3, G.4, G.6, R.4, and R.11.

Further Readings:

Guttman, Jon. *Caudron G.3*. Berkhamsted, UK: Albatros Publications, 2002.

No. 16: French Tanks Going Into Line

The tank made its debut on the battlefield in 1916, developed to overcome the machine gun. The first tanks were extremely slow, but would contribute significantly to ending the stalemate of trench warfare in the later stage of the war.

Further Readings:

Gale, Tim. *French Army's Tank Force and Armoured Warfare in the Great War*. London/New York: Routledge, 2016.

Gale, Tim. *French Tanks of the Great War: Development, Tactics and Operations*. Barnsley: Pen & Sword, 2016.

Glanfield, John. *The Devils' Chariots: The Birth and Secret Battles of the First Tanks*. London: Osprey, 2014.

No. 17 and 18: Inflating a French Sausage; German Plane Brought Down Near Nesle (Somme)

Observation balloons were common across the Western Front, allowing a peek over the trenches into the rear areas of one's enemy. The French called the observation balloon a "saucisse" (sausage) due to its shape.

Further Readings:

"Now Appears the Elephant of the Air," *Popular Science Monthly* 92, 4 (April 1918): 528.

No. 19: Camouflaged French Heavy [Artillery] on R.R. Car Near Vienne-Le-Chateau (Marne)

Some artillery guns, such as the well-known German "Dicke Bertha" (Big Bertha), were so heavy that they needed to be transported on railroad cars. It was an illusion, however, that big guns alone could end the war.

Vienne-le-Chateau- is 130 miles east of Paris.

Further Readings:

Severn, Mark. *The Gambardier: The Experiences of a Battery of Heavy Artillery on the Western Front During the First World War.* London: Leonaur, 2007.

No. 20 and 21: U.S.S. Lianga at Bordeaux; U.S.S. Rambler with Anti-Sub. Gun and Depth Bombs at Brest

The U.S.S. *West Lianga* (the caption records the name of the vessel incorrectly) was a cargo ship of the U.S. Navy, launched on 20 April 1918. Bordeaux had become the second most important supply port for U.S. forces in France by the end of the Great War, second only to Brest. The U.S.S. *Rambler* was a steam yacht that had been launched in 1900, but acquired for the U.S. Navy on 16 August 1917. It operated out of Brest and was used for patrol or escort duties, especially against German submarines.

Depth bombs, or depth charges, were explosives launched into the water in an effort to sink German submarines.

Further Readings:

Mooney, James L. *Dictionary of American Naval Fighting Ships*, 8 vols. Washington, D.C.: Navy Department, 1959-1981.

No. 22: French "220" Trench Mortar in Action

There was no 220 mm, but only the 240 mm Trench Mortar (Mortier de 240 mm CT), used by the French, Italian, and U.S. Army during the First World War, to be more precise between 1915 and 1918.

Further Readings:

United States Army. *Manual for Trench Artillery. Washington, D.C.*: Office of the Adjutant General, 1918.

No. 23 and 24: U.S. Coast Artillery in Action at Lenoncourt (Meuse); American Ambulance Service with French Army

This image was almost certainly taken in the same location as no. 13 above, though at a different time. It identifies the soldiers as being from the U.S. Coast Artillery Corps (CAC). Such units normally manned gun emplacements protecting major American port cities, but during the war many of these soldiers were deployed to France, where they operated a wide variety of artillery weapons, from anti-aircraft to railroad guns. The soldiers in this photograph, operating a howitzer, are likely of the 44th Artillery, CAC.

Before the American entry into the First World War, several thousand idealistic young Americans volunteered to serve the Allies through the American Field Service (AFS). Founded in 1915, the AFS performed numerous medical services in France (and later Italy), including driving ambulances in combat zones. With the U.S. declaration of war in 1917, the ambulance companies were brought into the American military command as the United States Army Ambulance Service, though these units typically still served with Allied armies. In addition to the AFS, many Americans volunteered to drive ambulances for the American Red Cross and the Norton-Hartjes Ambulance Corps. Among the more notable American ambulance drivers during the war were E.E. Cummings (1894-1962), John Dos Passos (1896-1970), and Ernest Hemingway (1899-1961).

Further Readings:

Berhow, Mark A. *American Seacoast Defenses: A Reference Guide*. 2nd ed. McLean, VA: CDSG Press, 2004.

Smucker, John M. *History of the United States Ambulance Service with the French and Italian Armies, 1917-1918-1919*. Allentown, PA: Schlechter, 1967.

No. 25: French Artillery Observation Post Near Vendresse (Aisne)

Artillery Fire Observers were "Fire Support Specialists" who were supposed to guide or command attacks by the own guns against the enemy lines. Vendresse is a commune in the Ardennes, 140 miles northeast of Paris.

No. 26 and 27: 155's in Action East of Rove; French Tank Leading an Attack Along Marne.

The French Canon de 155mm GPF (Grande Puissance Filloux) was invented by the French officer Louis Jean François Filloux (1869-1957) and introduced into the French Army in 1917 and later also used by the U.S. Army.

Further Readings:

Filloux, Louis. *Miscellaneous Notes Relative to the Materiel of the 155 G.P.F.* N.p., 1917.

No. 28: Wiring (Barbed) a Communication Trench (Oise)

Barbed wire originated in the late-nineteenth-century United States as a method to contain livestock on the Western frontier, but by the early twentieth century military forces around the world discovered its utility as a protective field barrier, and it became an iconic image of the First World War. During the Great War barbed wire was commonly used to secure positions against a possible enemy intrusion, as seen in this photograph, to protect the communication lines through a "communication trench" – one usually used by messengers to transport orders from the headquarters to the frontline positions. The trenches were, however, also used to transport supplies and to bring new troops to these positions.

Further Readings:

Razac, Oliver. *Barbed Wire: A Political History*. New York: New Press, 2002.

No. 29 and 30: Trench Scene at Bataglan, "Four de Paris" [Oven of Paris]; French First Aid Station

The trench became the natural environment for the combat soldiers of the First World War. A great number of men developed depression while at the front, and longed for a chance to get to a First Aid Station for a little relief from this melancholic life. Some even shot or mutilated themselves in order to leave the trenches. Frontline troops also rotated in and out of the trenches to preserve the morale and the sanity of the combat soldier.

Further Readings:

Asworth, Tony. *Trench Warfare, 1914-1918. The Live and Let Live System.* London: Pan Books, 2000.

Derren, Marie. "'Entrenched from Life': The Impossible Reintegration of Traumatized French Veterans of the Great War." In: *Psychological Trauma and the Legacies of the First World War,* eds. Jason Crouthamel and Peter Leese, 193-214. London: Palgrave, 2017.

Ellis, John. *Eye Deep in Hell: Trench Warfare in World War I.* Reprint. Baltimore, MD. John Hopkins University Press, 1989.

No. 31: At Practice with R[ed] C[ross] Dogs in the Trenches Near Luippes (Marne)

While seldom mentioned, animals played an important role during the Great War and the so called Red Cross dogs, to give just one example, were used to find or reach wounded soldiers in the field.

Further Readings:

Brouwer, Sigmund. *Innocent Heroes: Stories of Animals in the First World War*. Toronto: Tundra Books, 2017.

Pöppinghege, Rainer. *Tiere im Ersten Weltkrieg: Eine Kulturgeschichte*. Berlin: Rotbuch, 2014.

No. 32 and 33: French Artillery Observation Post; French Front Line Trenches

Very often, the soldiers could literally only "wait and see."

No. 34: French Troops Going to Front Line Thru Communications Trench

During a typical assault, the job of a frontline soldier was usually pretty clear – climb over the parapet of your trench, charge across "no man's land" toward the enemy, and seize his trench – but machine guns and artillery made it virtually impossible to accomplish the mission. Ten million would be dead by the time the war was over, often as a result of such futile attacks.

No. 35 and 36: Camouflaged Road Near Livry sur Vesle (Marne); French Heavy Artillery in Winter

Due to the increasing range of the heavy artillery more and more strategic targets needed to be camouflaged by the soldiers, who also had to live through harsh weather conditions in the autumn and winter months of the war years.

Livry-sur-Vesle, now Livry-Louvercy, is located fifteen miles southeast of Reims.

No. 37: Fritz "Fini" Near Belloy (Oise)

Marhefka's postcards seem to have an unusually large number of postcards depicting dead German soldiers. In this case, it is a dead German soldier, a "finished" (fini) man stereotypically called Fritz.

If the German enemy is mentioned or depicted in Marhefka's collection, he is either captured, dead, or named as responsible for some kind of destruction. The human side of the Germans is rarely shown. Such a one-sided view of the Germans is undoubtedly a reflection of the raw emotions in France (and among French postcard makers) in the immediate aftermath of the war. It also seems that Marhefka specifically selected such images, suggesting his own negative attitudes toward Germany and its people.

Belloy is a commune in northern France, sixty miles north of Paris.

No. 38 and 39: German First Aid Station — Forest of Ourchamf (Oise); Camouflaged German Battery Near Ostend

Ourchamf is a forest in the Département Oise, north of Paris. Ostend is a Belgian city on the North Sea.

No. 40: Near Soissons: German Machine Guns After the Fight

Soissons, located sixty miles northeast of Paris, was on near the frontlines throughout the war and saw considerable bloodshed. The area witnessed particularly bloody fighting during the ill-fated French offensives in the Chemin des Dames region in 1917. On 18 July 1918, American and French forces launched a major attack in the area. In three days, U.S. forces successfully severed the Soissons to Château-Thierry highway, but suffered more than 10,000 dead, wounded, or missing in the process. The specific offensive in which these German soldiers were killed is not noted.

The machine gun was one of the deadliest weapons during the Great War, especially since just a few men were able to defend a large area against an assault with this weapon. Many soldiers were consequently hit by a large number of bullets before they could even reach the enemy's line.

Further Readings:

Coppard, George. *With a Machine Gun to Cambrai.* Second Edition. London: Papermac, 1986.

Crutchley, C.E. *Machine Gunner 1914-1918: Personal Experiences of the Machine Gun Corps.* Barnsley: Pen & Sword, 2013.

No. 41 and 42: Boche Soldiers Near Roye (Oise); Remains of a Boche

The French used the term "boche" during the Great War to refer to their German opponents – usually as an insult. The term was originally used to address someone who is stubborn, but became emblematic for the German enemy during the 19th century. Americans sometimes used the term as well.

Further Readings:

Roynette, Odile. *Les mots des tranchées: l'invention d'une langue de guerre 1914-1919.* Paris: A. Colin, 2010.

No. 43: Dead Boche at Mouth of Abri.

"Abri" is the French term for shelter.

No. 44 and 45: Street in Noyon Mined by Germans; Ruins of Church at Ablain St. Nazaire (P de C)

The images show that cities were also tremendously transformed by the war. They could either become a war zone, where mines would keep the enemy away from strategically important spots (44) or destroyed by heavy artillery fire (45). Many postcards related to the Great War usually show soldiers posing in front of destroyed villages or buildings. Noyon and Ablain-Saint-Nazaire are both communes in northern France.

No. 46: A Destroyed Boche Stronghold (Somme)

The longer the war lasted, the more work was invested in strengthening the own trench positions. Many remnants of World War I trenches are still visible in the landscape today. The German "stronghold" depicted on this photograph is just one of countless examples.

No. 47 and 48: Remains of R.R. Bridge Over Marne Near Chateau Thierr[y]; Ruined Homes at Chateau Thierry

Château-Thierry looms large in the American experience of the First World War. On 27 May 1918, the Germans launched Operation Blücher-

Yorck in the Chemin des Dames region northeast of Paris, threatening the French capital. The Marne River was a major barrier to the German advance, and two bridges spanned the river at Château-Thierry, making it a tempting target for the Germans. Despite a lack of preparation and experience, the U.S. Third Division was thrown into the fight on 31 May and in the subsequent days and weeks played a significant role in preventing the Germans from crossing the river. For Americans, Château-Thierry symbolized the U.S. contribution to the Allied war effort, and demonstrated the fighting ability of the doughboy. After the battle, the Third Division assumed the moniker "Rock of the Marne," which it proudly bears to this day. The series of battles that took place along the Marne that summer are collectively known as the Second Battle of the Marne, and occurred not far from the critical fighting of 1914.

The first photograph shows the destruction of one of the two bridges at Château-Thierry. (The other bridge appears in images no. 51 and no. 57 below). The second highlights the result of the bitter fighting that took place across the city. As a representation of American participation in the war, images of U.S. battlefields such as these were highly popular among doughboy postcard collectors, and local French manufacturers produced them specifically for the American soldier market.

Further Readings:

Bonk, David and Peter Dennis. *Château Thierry & Belleau Wood 1918: America's Baptism of Fire on the Marne.* New York: Osprey, 2007.

Ralphson, G. Harvey. *Over There with the Marines at Chateau Thierry.* Chicago: M.A. Donohue & Co., 1919.

No. 49: German Cemetery Blown Up by Shell

Even the dead were not safe from the destructive power of artillery on the Western Front. The image suggests the ever-present atmosphere of death and destruction.

No. 50 and 51: Bridge at Mousson; Bridge at Chateau-Thierry Built Up by Americans

Pont-a-Mousson is located on the Moselle River. Many American volunteer ambulance companies served in the area before 1917, and U.S. troops saw action in the hills outside of town in the final days of the war, including the 92nd Division – a racially segregated African American unit. The second image shows the main bridge at Château-Thierry, repaired after the battles of May and June 1918.

No. 52: Explosion of German Time Bomb in Cambria (Nord)

This is a rare image of an explosion as it occurred. In the caption, "Cambria" is most likely a misspelling of Cambrai, a French city about 100 miles northeast of Paris, where significant fighting took place.

No. 53 and 54: Roye (Somme); U.S. Cemetery at Belleau Wood

The Battle of Belleau Wood, fought between 1 and 26 June 1918 was part of the Second Battle of the Marne. U.S. Marines attacked German positions in the woods on 6 June 1918 across open ground. They took enormous casualties, but gained a foothold in the woods. It took several more weeks of exceptionally bloody fighting, but the Marines ultimately prevailed. The U.S. troops counted almost 10,000 casualties, of which more than 1,800 were killed.

At the end of World War I, there were 75,636 American dead, whose remains were buried in more than 1,700 locations – most close to where they fell. After the war, the vast majority of the U.S. dead were disinterred and returned to the United States. Those who remained in Europe were gathered into eight overseas U.S. military cemeteries, such as the Aisne-Marne American Cemetery, which lies adjacent to Belleau Wood. Depicted in this postcard is one of the many battlefield cemeteries in the area around Belleau Wood, possibly now part of the Aisne-Marne American Cemetery.

Roye is seventy miles north of Paris.

Further Readings:

Moore, Ray T. *With the Marines at Belleau Wood: A Vivid Description of Personal Experiences in Battle.* Wake Forest, N.C.: Euzelian Society, 1921.
Suskind, Richard. *The Battle of Belleau Wood.* New York: Macmillan, 1969.
Dickon, Chris. *The Foreign Burial of American War Dead.* Jefferson, NC: McFarland, 2011.

No. 55: Rheims — Cathedral in Background

Rheims, today more commonly spelled Reims, was heavily shelled by the German artillery during the war, and the city's famed cathedral, where French kings were once crowned, was heavily damaged. Its height provided a convenient landmark for German gunners sighting their guns. The ravaged cathedral would consequently become one of the main images in Allied anti-German propaganda during the Great War. Marhefka's postcard collection has numerous images of the Reims Cathedral. Others are below.

Further Readings:

Emery, Elizabeth. "The Martyred Cathedral: American Attitudes toward Notre-Dame de Reims During the First World War." In: *Medieval Art and Architecture after the Middle Ages*, eds. Janet T. Marquardt and Alyce A. Jordan, 312-339. Newcastle upon Tyne: Cambridge Scholars Publishing, 2011.

No. 56 and 57: Ham — Rue de Chauny; End of Bridge at Chateau Thierry Blown Up by Americans During German Drive

That cities were heavily damaged during the battles of the Great War is clearly visible in these photographs, which show the post-battle perspective of the urban environment. Here is yet another image of the destroyed bridge at Château-Thierry, suggesting the importance of the location in the American memory of the war. Incidentally, it was French engineers that blew the bridge at Château-Thierry in order to prevent German forces from crossing the river.

No. 58: On Board U.S.S. Rumpler — Ready for the Subs

The ship is, in fact, the U.S.S. Rambler. The vessel is shown in image no. 21 above, and was mainly used for patrol missions.

No. 59 and 60: Fords L.D. at M.T.C.R. Park #714, Bourg, France; Tree Felled by Shell at Pontavert (Oise)

The first image is a photographic print of Marhefka's duty station in Bourg, France, with the caption likely written by hand by Marhefka himself.

No. 61: Camp Américain de Bourg Hte Marne

This postcard of the Reception Park at Bourg was likely made locally for a very small customer base – the American troops, like Marhefka, working at the park. Undoubtedly taken in the summer of 1919, it shows the immense number of vehicles the U.S. Army shipped to the Bourg reception park, and the challenges Marhefka faced in his work there. The caption in French suggests that local residents may have purchased copies as well.

No. 62: Motors at Motors Reception Park #714, Bourg, France.

This image, along with the following seven, are photographic prints of the reception park at Bourg, indicating the daily routine of Motor Supply

Train No. 426 in disassembling obsolete vehicles and preparing them for resale or scrap. It is likely Marhefka wrote the captions for each image on the page below the image, and it is conceivable he even took the photographs himself.

No. 63: Radiators at Motor Reception Park #714, Bourg, France

No. 64: Solid Rubber Tire Wheels at Motor Reception Park #714, Bourg, France

No. 65: Wheels and Rims at Motor Reception Park #714, Bourg, France

No. 66: Differentials at Motor Reception Park #714, Bourg, France

No. 67: Ford Rear Axels [sic] at Motor Reception Park #714, Bourg, France

No. 68: Skid and Drag Chains at Motor Reception Park #714, Bourg, France

No. 69: Motors at Motor Reception Park #714, Bourg, France

No. 70: American Cemetery at France [sic]

This image appears to be a postcard print of an unidentified American cemetery. Marhefka likely wrote the caption himself, and seems to have left a blank space for the location of the cemetery, then – for whatever reason – never wrote it in. In addition to combat deaths, 63,114 Americans died of diseases, accidents, and other causes. Before the consolidation of the American war dead, there were U.S. cemeteries all across France, including one in Neufchâteau, one at Bazoilles, and two in Langres. These photographs may have been taken at one of those locations.

Further Readings:

United States War Department. *Location of Graves and Disposition of Bodies of American Soldiers Who Died Overseas*. Washington: Government Printing Office, 1920.

No. 71: American Cemetery at France

This image is remarkably similar to no. 70 above.

No. 72: Liberty Trucks at Motor Reception Park #714, Bourg, France

The Standard B "Liberty" Truck was used by the U.S. Army during the Great War. Designed by the U.S. Army Quartermaster Corps, it was the workhorse of the Motor Transport Corps.

Further Readings:

Mroz, Albert. *American Military Vehicles of World War I*. Jefferson, NC: McFarland, 2009.

No. 73: 10,000 German dead — Verdun — 1918

The largest and longest battle of the Great War was the Battle of Verdun, fought between 21 February and 18 December 1916. With a total of around 300,000 dead soldiers (more than 140,000 Germans and more than 150,000 French) it is not surprising, that those who had to fight there referred to the Verdun as the "blood pump" or "bone mill." This photograph, taken a couple of years after that awful struggle, seems to confirm the soldiers' observations.

Further Readings:

Brown, Malcolm. *Verdun 1916*. Stroud: Tempus, 2003.

Horne, Alistair. *Verdun 1916*. London: Penguin Books, 2007.

Jessen, Olaf. *Verdun 1916. Urschlacht des Jahrhunderts*. Munich: Beck, 2014.

Prost, Antoine and Gerd Krumeich. *Verdun 1916: Une histoire franco-allemande de la bataille*. Paris: Talandier, 2015.

Frank Marhefka's Postcard Collection

No. 74. 75, and 76: German Cemetary [sic] Drancourt, Champagne; To the End; and Hindenburg Line (Soissons)

It seems like Marhefka (or at least those who produced the cards he collected) wanted to portray the pointless resistance of the German soldiers who defended the Hindenburg Line "To the End," just to be either left in the field or to lie six feet under in a cemetery in northern France.

The Hindenburg Line or *Siegfriedstellung* was the German defensive position in the winter 1916/17, near Soissons on the Aisne.

Further Readings:

Geyer, Michael. "Rückzug und Zerstörung 1917." In: *Die Deutschen an der Somme 1914-1918: Krieg, Besatzung und verbrannte Erde*, eds. Gerhard Hirschfeld, Gerd Krumeich, and Irina Renz, 163-179. Essen: Klartext, 2006.

No. 77: U.S. Troops at Hill 204 — Belleau Wood

Hill 204 looms above the Marne River between Château-Thierry and Belleau Wood. On 1 July 1918, a Franco-American force began an attack that eventually drove the Germans from the position. U.S. forces concentrated in the village of Vaux at the base of the hill. Today, Hill 204 is the location of the Château-Thierry American Monument.

No. 78 and 79: Ruined House Soissons and Church Arras

The two photographs show the level of destruction in Soissons and Arras, two cities in northern France.

No. 80: German Bodies and Dugout

More dead Germans.

No. 81, 82, and 83: German's Entertainment; Rheims, Town Hall; Ruined Belgium Village

An interesting grouping of images. The first shows the humanity of the German enemy. Juxtaposed with it are two others suggesting the destruction visited upon France and Belgium by German soldiers like these.

No. 84: Dead Germans (Oise)

No. 85 and 86: Practical Use Made of Boche Helmet; A Friendly Game

The realities of war became daily life for the soldiers, who had to make the best out of this situation. While there were not many happy moments due to the trench warfare, there also have been short times of pleasure, as these photographs document. Note that the soldiers in the second image are wearing the distinctive Montana Peak campaign hat, indicating that these soldiers at play are American.

No. 87: Boches Ready to Be Buried Chateau Thierry

After the battle it was time to bury friend and foe alike.

Frank Marhefka's Postcard Collection

No. 88 and 89: Moving Into An Advanced Position; Belleau Wood — Germans After the Fight

No. 90: Germans in Belleau Wood

This image purports to show German soldiers attacking toward the position of the photographer. If authentic, it is a rare example of a photograph taken in action.

No. 91 and 92: Chateau Thierry; American Camp Hospital

If wounded at the front, soldiers on all sides passed through a complex chain of medical facilities. For U.S. casualties, there were field medics at the front who brought the wounded to aid posts just behind the lines. From there, the wounded were evacuated to a field hospital, where they were triaged based on severity of wounds and received surgical care if needed. Those requiring more elaborate operations and/or rehabilitation were then evacuated to larger and more comprehensive hospitals in a rear area. By the end of the war, the AEF had a network of 231 hospitals across France, Belgium, Italy, and the United Kingdom.

Further Reading:

Lynch, Charles G., ed. *The Medical Department of the United States Army in the World War*, 17 vols. Washington: GPO, 1921-1929.

No. 93: After the Marne Fighting (1914-1916)

The First Battle of the Marne, 6-10 September 1914, forced the German Army to stop its advance into France, but caused an extremely high number of casualties — Holger Herwig estimated 300,000 for all participating armies.

Further Reading:

Herwig, Holger. *The Marne, 1914: The Opening of World War I and the Battle that Changed the World.* New York: Random House, 2009.

No. 94 and 95: U.S. Trench Mortar; Receiving Instruction in Use of Rifle Grenades

The U.S. government did not declare war before 1917, and it took time for the troops to enter the fighting stage of the Great War. In the meantime, the doughboys had to learn a lot of things by doing them in the field.

No. 96: Rheims

Another image of the famous cathedral: Reims was battered but never fell, and to Marhefka and other Allied soldiers, such a postcard likely symbolized steadfastness and triumph in the face of German attacks. In 1962, French President Charles de Gaulle (1890-1970) and West German Chancellor Konrad Adenauer (1876-1967) re-dedicated that cathedral to the spirit of Franco-German reconciliation.

No. 97 and 98: Street in Rheims After the Bombardment; Interior View Rheims Cathedral

These images, which witnessed the destruction of "French culture" by "German barbarism" were widely circulated.

No. 99: Rheims Cathedrale

This image appears to be a reproduction of a standard tourist postcard. For American troops who might never have seen such massive and ornate sacred buildings before, medieval cathedrals like the one at Reims must have been very impressive.

No. 100 and 101: A Steaming Field Kitchen Headed Toward the Front; An A.E.F. Kitchen

Another logistical task that needed to be mastered during the war: "How to feed the soldiers?"

No. 102: Occupying a New Position

World War I is famous for the static trench warfare on the Western Front, but the war most American combat troops experienced in 1918 was often one of movement, as armies on both sides of the Western Front had learned to overcome their entrenched opponents by that time. This image might well be staged or taken during training. Note, for example, that the photographer's point of view is above the parapet of the embankment behind which the soldiers are lined up – a very dangerous position in the midst of combat.

No. 103 and 104: French Battery of 155's in Woods; A "370" in Action

The 370 mm was a French railway howitzer, used during the Great War. To strengthen its artillery, the French Army employed coastal defense batteries in the land war. These guns were transported to the Western Front by rail.

Further Reading:

Miller, Harry W. *Railway Artillery*, 2 vols. Washington, D.C.: Government Printing Office, 1921.

No. 105: Belleau Wood Amer[ican] Cemetary [sic]

This is an image of one of many temporary U.S. battlefield cemeteries in the area around Belleau Wood.

No. 106 and 107: German Cannon at Zeebrugge; French Tanks

Zeebrugge is a village on the Belgian coast and today serves as the modern port for Bruges.

In the Zeebrugge Raid of 23 April 1918, British forces sank obsolete ships at the mouth of the harbor in an attempt to block German ships and submarines from entering and leaving the port. The raid did indeed hinder German operations, though only temporarily. Both sides claimed victory in this unusual encounter.

Further Reading:

Kendall, Paul. *The Zeebrugge Raid 1918: The Finest Feat of Arms.* Stroud: History Press, 2009.

No. 108: German Camp

No. 109, 110, and 111: Argonne Wood; Argonne Forest (1918); Argonne Forest

The Meuse-Argonne Offensive of 1918 was the largest American operation of the First World War. It commenced on 26 September 1918, in coordination with British, French, and Belgian forces, as part of Marshal Foch's "Grand Offensive" to end the war. By the time it ended with the armistice of 11 November 1918, the operation had involved 1.2 million doughboys, of whom 26,000 had been killed. Some of the heaviest and most difficult fighting of the campaign occurred in the Argonne Forest, on the extreme left of the U.S. front, where the 77th Division (made up mainly of draftees from New York City) had the unenviable task of pushing back the Germans through rugged and heavily forested hills. One group, the so-called "Lost Battalion," was pinned down by German forces for a week before their comrades could reach them. For Americans, the Argonne Forest represented the worst of what World War I had to offer.

The three images of the Argonne Forest in Marhefka's postcard collection are rare combat photographs, likely taken from an airplane, that somehow got into the hands of a postcard producer. They emphasize that the Great War not only destroyed countless lives, but also the natural environment.

Further Readings:

Keller, Tait. "Destruction of the Ecosystem." In: *1914-1918-online. International Encyclopedia of the First World War*, ed. by Ute Daniel, Peter Gatrell, Oliver Janz, Heather Jones, Jennifer Keene, Alan Kramer, and Bill Nasson, issued by Freie Universität Berlin, Berlin 2014-10-08. Accessed August 19, 2018. https://encyclopedia.1914-1918-online.net/article/destruction_of_the_ecosystem

Lengel, Edward. *To Conquer Hell: The Meuse-Argonne, 1918*. New York: Holt, 2008.

Slotkin, Richard. *Lost Battalions: The Great War and the Crisis of American Nationality*. New York: Holt, 2005.

No. 112: Americans Attacking at Cantigny Lead by French Tank

Cantigny is a village in the Picardy region of France, 73 miles northeast of Paris. On 28 May 1918, the U.S. Army launched its first significant offensive of the war against German forces in the village. The United States had been in the war for more than a year, but had seen little action. British and French officials questioned the combat effectiveness of America's inexperienced troops. At Cantigny the U.S. First Division took the village that morning, then held it against German counterattacks for several days. Though the operation was limited in scope, it dispelled fears that the American army could not fight.

This photograph shows U.S. troops advancing with the support of French tanks, prefiguring the mobile, combined arms warfare that emerged late in the First World War and would typify the Second World War two decades later.

Further Reading:

Weingartner, Steven, ed. *Cantigny at Seventy-Five: A Professional Discussion.* Chicago: Robert R. McCormick Tribune Foundation, 1994.

Frank Marhefka's Postcard Collection

No. 113, 114, and 115: Trench St. Mihiel; French Going Over the Top Chateau Thierry; Smoke Barrage

These three images seem to come from the same maker as the Argonne Forest postcards above. This producer seemed to specialize in combat images. Two once again appear to be aerial shots. A smoke barrage was often laid down before an infantry assault to conceal the movement of advancing troops.

No. 116: Nieuport "Chasse" Plane

No. 117, 118, and 119: German machine gunners retreating (Belleau Wood); German flames [sic] throwers; German trenches (Belleau Wood)

Three more postcards purported to be combat images, though some may be of training exercises. Note the high mountains in the background of the first image, for example, which are unlike the landscape in the Belleau Wood area.

No. 120: Fourth of July in Paris – 1918

A year before, on 4 July 1917, U.S. troops had marched through the streets of the French capital to the grave of Marquis de Lafayette (1757-1834), a French officer, who had served in the American Revolutionary War. In 1918, with the war almost at an end, the U.S. troops again paraded through the capital of France.

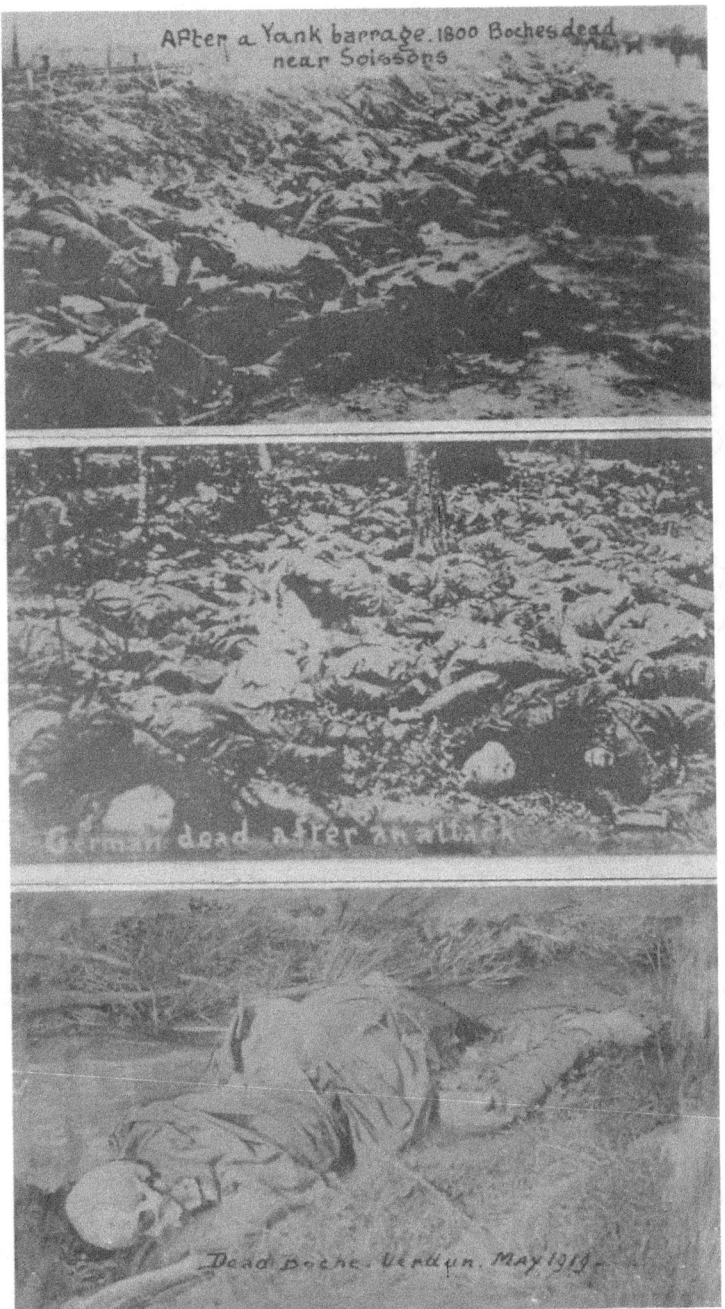

No. 121, 122 and 123: After a Yank Barrage: 1800 Boches Dead Near Soissons; German Dead after an Attack; Dead Boche, Verdun, May 1919.

For many soldiers, photographs of enemy dead likely represented their pride in triumph over the enemy, or perhaps their own survival in the horrific events of the war.

No. 124: German Prisoners (Marne)

During the war, all sides displayed captured enemy equipment, or "war trophies," to symbolize their triumph. Parading captured enemy soldiers, like the Germans being marched through an unidentified French city, served the same purpose. During the war, prisoners were put to work on labor details, and were a common sight on military bases and other areas behind the lines.

Further Reading:

Yarnell, John. *Barbed Wire Disease: British and German Prisoners of War, 1914-1919* Stroud, England: The History Press, 2011.

No. 125, 126, and 127: Dead Boche (Amiens); Wo[u]nded Boche (Argonne); Dead Boche (Chateau-Thierry)

It is remarkable, that Marhefka, who rather collected images of weapons, buildings, and new technologies in the first part of his album, showed a growing interest in corpses and dead enemies the longer he spent time abroad during the conflict. This "collection habit" is of particular interest. Marhefka was never in combat, yet still he collected all these images of dead enemy soldiers. One has to wonder, why this was important for his collection, or "recreation" of his memory of the war.

Further Reading:

Mosse, George L. *Fallen Soldiers: Reshaping the Memory of the World Wars.* Oxford/New York: Oxford University Press, 1991.

No. 128: German Observation Balloon

A photograph of another "flying sausage."

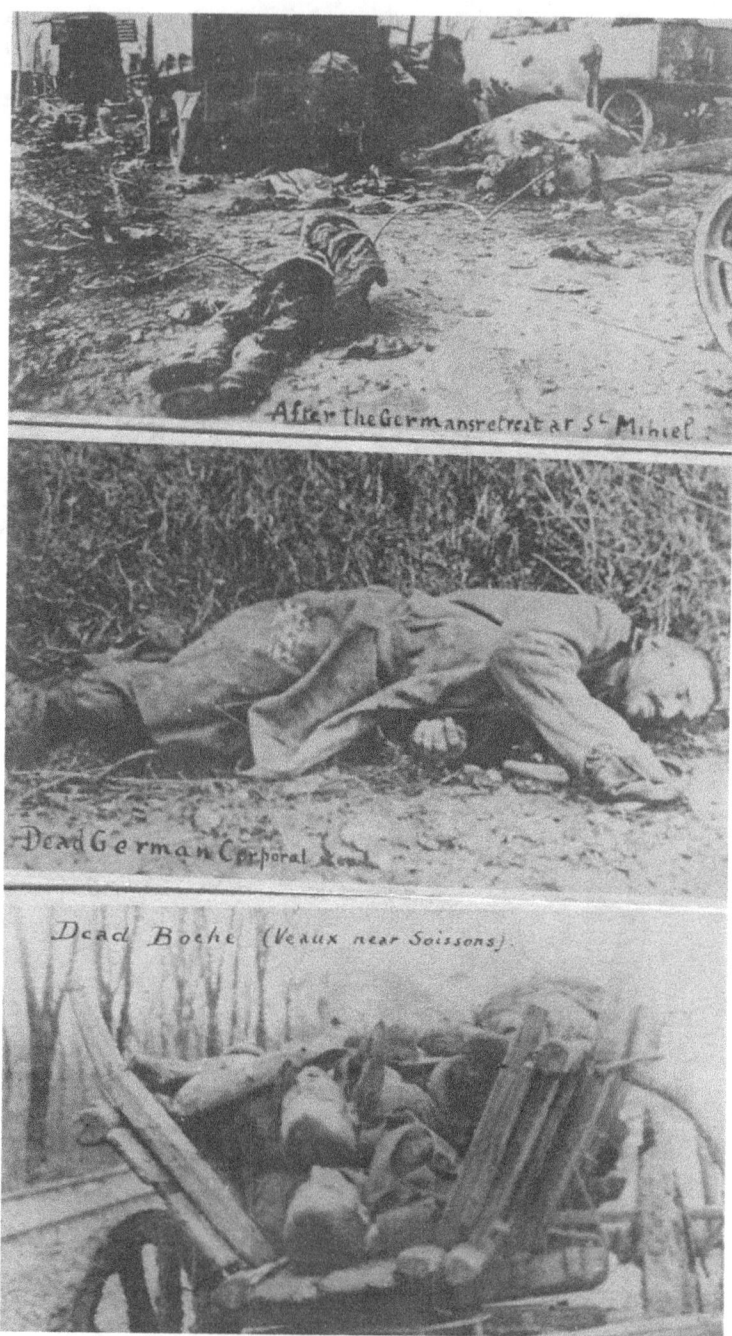

No. 129, 130, and 131: After the Germans Retreated at St. Mihiel; Dead German Corporal; Dead Boche (Veaux near Soissons)

Three more images of dead Germans: The Battle of Saint-Mihiel between 12 and 15 September 1918, involved the soldiers of the American Expeditionary Force and more than 100,000 French soldiers under the command of General Pershing. It was the first major American offensive of the war, and was a stunning success – though German soldiers had already begun an evacuation back to a more defensible line when the offensive began.

Further Readings:

Bonk, David. *St. Mihiel 1918: The American Expeditionary Forces' Trial by Fire*. London: Osprey, 2011.

Hallas, James H. *Squandered Victory: The American First Army at St. Mihiel*. Santa Barbara, CA: Praeger, 1995.

No. 132: U.S. Artillery Moving Into Position

Frank Marhefka's Postcard Collection

No. 133, 134, and 135: St. Mihiel bridge Cheroncourt; Mine Explosion Cheroncourt; German Planes Raid, Paris (July 1918), Boulevard Voltaire

More scenes of destruction.

No. 136: Firing a Heavy C.A.C.

This image is likely a different angle from the U.S. coast artillery unit shown in postcards no. 13 and no. 23 above.

No. 137, 138, and 139: Ruins near St. Mihiel; Chateau Thierry — Town Hall; Bombarded House Grandpré

The destructive power of the Great War seemed to have hit almost every town in northern France and Marhefka's postcards document the path of destruction. Grandpré is located 130 miles east of Paris.

No. 140: German Anti-Air-Craft Gun

This photograph is almost certainly staged. Note the shadow of the photographer.

No. 141, 142, and 143: German Gun; Big German Gun (Crépy-en-Laonnois); and French Flames [sic] Thrower

Flamethrowers were also a weapon of the First World War that was widely used. While the technology per se had already been used by the Greeks ("Greek Fire") in the first century C.E., the modern flamethrower was invented by the German scientist Richard Fiedler in 1905.

Crépy-en-Laonnois is located ninety miles northeast of Paris.

Further Readings:

McNab, Chris. *The Flamethrower*. London: Bloomsbury, 2015.

Wictor, Thomas. *German Flamethrower Pioneers of World War I*. Atglen, PA: Schiffer, 2007.

No. 144: Kaiser, Von Kluck, Crownprinz. G.H.Q.

General Alexander von Kluck (1846-1934) commanded the German First Army until he was wounded in late 1915.

Wilhelm (1882-1951) was Crown Prince and the oldest son of Wilhelm II.

No. 145, 146, and 147: British Tank Disguised by Huns (Champagne); Wrecked Airplane (Toul); Wrecked Airplane (Marne)

These three images depict the most advanced weapons World War I had to offer. Germany was slow to adopt the tank, often using captured British models. Ironically, in World War II Germany mastered both the airplane and the tank, and the art of combined arms warfare with blitzkrieg.

The Germans were often referred to as "Huns" in Allied propaganda, suggesting a non-existent connection between Attila the Hun (406-453), who invaded Europe in ancient times, and the modern German nation. Toul is located 170 miles east of Paris.

No. 148: Suresnes, American Cemetary [sic]. President Wilson. MEMORIAL Day. May 30th 1919.

Woodrow Wilson (1856-1924) was the American president during the First World War. In January 1918 he unveiled a peace plan called the Fourteen Points. Included in Wilson's proposals was an international organization he hoped would preserve world peace called the League of Nations – forerunner of today's United Nations. Wilson firmly believed that American engagement was necessary for a lasting peace, and he even traveled to the peace negotiations at Versailles, France personally. Unfortunately for Wilson, many of his peace proposals went unrealized. Ironically, the Allies voted to create the League of Nations, but the U.S. Congress refused to ratify the treaty, so the United States would not participate. Instead, the United States chose a unilateral path in foreign affairs after the war.

While in Paris, Wilson attended the dedication of an American military cemetery at Suresnes, a Paris suburb. This cemetery contained the dead from the many U.S. military hospitals in the Paris area, as well as those who had fallen victim to accident or disease behind the lines. The dedication occurred on American Memorial Day, then commemorated on 30 May but now on the fourth Monday in May.

Further Readings:

Berg, A. Scott. *Wilson*. New York: Putnam, 2013.

Cooper, John Milton, Jr. *Breaking the Heart of the World: Woodrow Wilson and the Fight for the League of Nations*. New York: Cambridge University Press, 2001.

Striner, Richard. *Woodrow Wilson and World War I: A Burden Too Great to Bear*. Lanham, MD: Rowman & Littlefield, 2014.

No. 149, 150, and 151: Amer[ican] Doughboys on Review; Blue Devils Saluting Amer[ican] Flag; First Amer[ican]s on Parade, June 1917 (Bois de Boulogne)

These three images of U.S. soldiers are most likely from the same producer as the goriest battlefield images in this collection. The Blue Devils was the nickname of the U.S. 88th Division, which arrived in France too late to see any action in World War I. The Bois de Boulogne is a large park on the west side of Paris.

Since the time of the Mexican-American War (1846-1848) U.S. soldiers were named doughboys. One story claims that troops, who had been marching through the Mexican desert areas, looked like covered in dough, why they were named "doughboys" later. During the First World War, it was already common to call U.S. infantry soldiers that way.

Further Reading:

Larson, E.D.J. *Memoirs of France and the Eighty-eighth Division: Being a Review Without Official Character of the Experiences of the "Cloverleaf" Division in the Great World War from 1917 to 1919.* Minneapolis: privately published, 1920.

Keene, Jennifer. *World War I: The American Experience.* Lincoln: University of Nebraska Press, 2011.

No. 152: Von Hindenburg

Paul von Hindenburg (1847-1934) was the leader of the German High Command (*Oberste Heeresleitung*) and during the second period of the war controlled not only the Imperial Army, but also German politics. His role for the further political course of the Weimar Republic was decisive, as he served as President of Germany between 1925 and 1934.

Further Reading:

Pyta, Wolfram. *Hindenburg: Herrschaft zwischen Hohenzollern und Hitler.* Munich: Siedler, 2007.

Frank Marhefka's Postcard Collection

No. 153, 154, and 155: French & Ameri[can]s Reviewing Troops; French Soldiers Being Decorated; Krownprinz at Soissons

The first two images are likely by the same postcard maker as images no. 149-151 above, and possibly taken of the same military parade.

Friedrich Wilhelm Victor August Ernst (1882-1951), Crown Prince of Prussia and Germany, was the first son of Wilhelm II (1859-1941). He formally commanded the Fifth German Army during the war, including the Battle of Verdun.

No. 156: The King of Saxonie

Frederick Augustus III (1865-1932) was the last king of the House of Wettin, who ruled Saxony until he – due to the German Revolution of 1918 – "voluntarily" abdicated on 13 November 1918.

Frank Marhefka's Postcard Collection

No. 157 and 158: [No descriptions]

These two images are unlabeled, and may be snapshots rather than postcards. They appear to show soldier dugouts. The appearance of two women (who are likely nurses or welfare workers) in the first image suggests the photograph was taken after the cessation of hostilities. Tourists began to flock to the battlefields almost immediately after the cessation of hostilities, and probably purchased postcards such as those Marhefka collected. It is possible that Marhefka might have visited battle sites after the war, though there is no evidence of it.

No. 159: American Cemetery in Romagne Near Verdun (France)

The Meuse-Argonne American Cemetery near Romagne-sous-Montfaucon is the largest of the eight U.S. cemeteries constructed in Europe after World War I. It was at this spot on 14 October 1918, that American forces broke through the *Kriemhilde Stellung*, a major German fortification line between the Argonne Forest and the Meuse River. The breakthrough severely undermined the German position in the area, forcing their retreat northward. Three weeks later, the war was over. The cemetery today contains the remains of 14,276 American service members, including 486 unknown soldiers, twenty-one sets of brothers, and nine Medal of Honor recipients. An additional 954 soldiers whose remains were never recorded are commemorated there as well. This postcard image shows the cemetery in its earliest stages of development. Marhefka likely placed it on the final page of his scrapbook as a poignant reminder of war's cost, and a tribute to fallen fellow Americans.

Epilogue

After the Great War, Frank Marhefka returned to Shamokin and went back to work as a salesman, first for a shoe company, then at a hardware store.[1] He married a local woman named Sara Spatzer shortly after the war, and together they had two children, Frank Leonard, Jr. and Mary Jane. The birth of Frank, Jr. in 1924 even made the front page of the *Shamokin Dispatch*, and the announcement suggested that elder Marhefka had become a well-known figure in town. The newspaper described the new arrival as "a lusty son, who already gives evidence of the inherited ability that has distinguished his father's service as an expert salesman."[2] Whatever Marhefka's persuasive abilities in sales may have been, the Great Depression seems to have put an end to his retail career. By the 1930s he was working as a silk finisher at the Eagle Silk Company, and spent the remainder of his working years in factory work.

In his leisure time, Marhefka enjoyed singing and theater, and regularly participated in Shamokin's annual minstrel show. "Blackface Production … Scores Heavily With Large Audience," announced a headline in the *Shamokin Dispatch* of the 1932 performance, in which Marhefka sang in the chorus.[3] His participation in the shows grew over the years. "The annual production is under the direction of Frank Marhefka," reported the *Dispatch* in 1937, "of many years successful experience in minstrel work."[4] Marhefka was also active in local veterans' affairs, particularly with the American Legion. Founded by doughboys in Paris in 1919, the American Legion became America's leading veterans' organization during the 1920s. Exclusively the domain of World War I veterans during the interwar period, the organization opened its membership to World War II veterans in the 1940s, and then extended it to nearly all veterans of U.S. military service by

---

[1] *Shamokin Dispatch*, April 29, 1924.

[2] Ibid.

[3] *Shamokin Dispatch*, April 13, 1932.

[4] *Shamokin Dispatch*, May 12 1937.

the end of the century.⁵ As an American Legion member, Marhefka took part in numerous local patriotic and commemorative events, and undoubtedly marched proudly in Memorial Day parades. In the early 1950s he served several terms the vice-commander of Shamokin's American Legion post, and was then elected post commander in 1955.⁶

After his retirement, Marhefka and his wife moved into the home of Frank, Jr. – a school principal – in Mifflintown, Pennsylvania. Sadly, declining health plagued his later years. Sara passed away on 4 October 1976,⁷ and Frank followed soon thereafter. He died on 24 June 1977. As his obituary in the *News-Item* of Shamokin noted, his passing came "after a long illness."⁸ He was buried in St. Stanislaus Cemetery in Shamokin, next to his parents and surrounded by family members.

***

For Frank Marhefka, World War I was probably the biggest event of his life (beyond his marriage or the birth of his children, of course) and his postcard collection was a souvenir of that extraordinary experience. People collect souvenirs for many reasons. One is to keep memories alive. Recollections fade over time, but a souvenir (derived from the French "to remember") helps perpetuate them – whether a photograph, a postcard image, or a three-dimensional artifact. Souvenirs help "locate, define, and freeze in time a fleeting, transitory experience," wrote Beverly Gordon.⁹ Leafing through his album of wartime postcards, Marhefka could think back to the people he met and the friendships he made during the war, and relive his travels through France – heady and remarkable stuff for a working class man from Shamokin.

However, souvenirs do more than just preserve memories. They also make statements. Perhaps, at the same time, Marhefka liked to show off his postcards to others, and if he did, he was communicating something about who he was and how he saw himself. He would have been announcing his role as an actor in one of history's great dramas – the First World War – even if it may have been a bit part. He would also have been making it known that he answered his nation's call to duty during a time of nation-

---

[5] For more on the American Legion, see William Pencak, *For God and Country: The American Legion, 1919-1941* (Boston: Northeastern University Press, 1989) and Thomas A. Rumer, *The American Legion: An Official History* (New York: Evans, 1990).

[6] *Shamokin Dispatch*, 21 June 1955.

[7] *News-Item* (Shamokin, PA), October 5, 1976.

[8] *News-Item* (Shamokin, PA), June 25, 1977.

[9] Beverly Gordon, "The Souvenir: Messenger of the Extraordinary," *Journal of Popular Culture* 20, 3 (1986): 135.

al emergency and therefore became a vivid part of the nation itself. Given his extensive involvement in the American Legion, Marhefka was clearly proud of his military service. "Much like peacetime travelers advertised their social status and through souvenirs," wrote Mark D. Van Ells in his study of souvenir collecting by American troops during the Second World War, "the GIs highlighted their special status as veterans and historical actors with mementoes of the military world."[10] The same could be said for the doughboys of the First World War – or participants in any war.

Marhefka's postcards show scenes of death and destruction that, as a supply sergeant in a motor supply train, he would probably not have witnessed himself. Why he collected such gruesome images is a matter of speculation. They might have reminded him as a survivor of the seminal catastrophe of the 20th century of the cruel side of war and he might have used them to warn his descendants as well. Especially the image of dead soldiers in Marhefka's collection had a clear message: In war, people get killed. Nevertheless, some people are simply attracted to the macabre. "The act of collecting souvenirs," observed the travel writer Rolf Potts, "has not always been an innocent ... expression."[11] Throughout military history, there have been those who have sliced away the body parts of their vanquished enemies – the ultimate victory trophy in the ultimate human contest. Though a non-combatant, Marhefka may have thought of these grisly postcards as his own kind of trophy, symbolizing his efforts in a difficult but victorious cause. Non-combat soldiers have long sought mementos from the battlefield, perhaps as a way to bask in the honor afforded to the combat veteran, or perhaps even as props to tell embellished or even fictional tales of their own wartime experiences. The most likely explanation is that Marhefka simply found these postcards inexpensive and widely available in France.

Souvenirs offer what Danielle Lasusa characterized as "proof of one's travels."[12] With his postcard album, Marhefka could prove that he had "been there" – an actor in history, serving his country in a time of war.

---

[10] Van Ells, "An Amazing Collection," forthcoming.

[11] Rolf Potts, *Souvenir* (New York: Bloomsbury, 2018), 65.

[12] Danielle M. Lasusa, "Eiffel Tower Key Chains and Other Pieces of Reality: The Philosophy of Souvenirs," *Philosophic Forum* 38, 3 (2007): 279.

Works Cited

Unpublished Sources

National Archives, College Park, Maryland.
 Records of the American Expeditionary Forces (RG 120)

National Archives, Washington, D.C.
 Records of the Selective Service System (Record Group 163)

Pennsylvania State Archives, Harrisburg, Pennsylvania
 Records of the Department of Military and Veterans Affairs (RG 19)

Periodicals

Mount Carmel Item
Shamokin Dispatch
News-Item (Shamokin, PA)

Published Works

Addison, James Thayer. *The Story of the First Gas Regiment*. Boston: Houghton Mifflin, 1919.

Allen, James, Hilton Als, Congressman John Lewis, and Leon F. Litwack. *Without Sanctuary: Lynching Photography in America*. Santa Fe, NM: Twin Palms Publishers, 2000.

Allied and Associated Powers (1914-1920). *Report of the Military Board of Allied Supply*. Washington: GPO, 1924-1925.

Anderson, Benedict. *Imagined Communities: Reflections on the Origin and Spread of Nationalism*, revised edition. London: Verso, 2016.

Andrews, James Henry Millar, Charles Elcock, and J.S. Bradford. *Soldiers of the Castle: A History of Company B, Engineer Battalion, National Guard of Pennsylvania, Afterward Company B, 103rd Engineers, 28th Division, A.E.F.* Philadelphia: Hoeflich Printing House, 1929.

Asworth, Tony. *Trench Warfare, 1914-1918. The Live and Let Live System*. London: Pan Books, 2000.

Bairnsfather, Bruce. *Fragments of France*. New York: G.P. Putnam, 1917.

-----. *More Fragments from France*. New York: G.P. Putman, 1918.

Bauer, Franz J. *Das "lange" 19. Jahrhundert (1789-1917): Profil einer Epoche*. Stuttgart: Reclam, 2004.

Bell, Herbert C. and J.J. John. *History of Northumberland County, Pennsylvania*. Chicago: Brown, Runk & Co., 1891.

Benoît, Christian. *Le canon de 75: Une gloire centenaire.* Vincennes: Service historique de l'Armée de terre, 1996.

Berg, A. Scott. *Wilson.* New York: Putnam, 2013.

Berhow, Mark A. *American Seacoast Defenses: A Reference Guide.* 2nd ed. McLean, VA: CDSG Press, 2004.

Beyrer, Klaus, ed. *Kommunikation im Kaiserreich: Der Generalpostmeister Heinrich von Stephan.* Heidelberg: Edition Braus, 1997.

Binot, Jean-Marc. *Georges Guynemer.* Paris: Fayard, 2017.

Bodgan, Robert and Todd Weseloh. *Real Photo Postcard Guide: The People's Photography.* Syracuse, NY: Syracuse University Press, 2006.

Bonk, David and Peter Dennis. *Château Thierry & Belleau Wood 1918: America's Baptism of Fire on the Marne.* New York: Osprey, 2007.

-----. *St. Mihiel 1918: The American Expeditionary Forces' Trial by Fire.* London: Osprey, 2011.

Bowers, Q. David. "Souvenir Postcards and the Development of the Star System, 1912-1914." *Film History* 3 (1989): 39-45.

Boyd's Directory of Shamokin: Containing the Names of the Citizens, Compendium of the Government and of Public and Private Institutions, 1901-1903. Reading, PA: W.H. Boyd, 1901.

Boyd's Directory of Shamokin: Containing the Names of the Citizens, A Compendium of the Government and of Public and Private Institutions, 1913-1915. Reading, PA: W.H. Boyd, 1913.

Boyd's Shamokin and Sunbury Directory: Containing the Names of the Citizens, a Compendium of the Government, and of Public and Private Institutions, 1886-1888. Pottsville, PA: W. Harry Boyd, 1886.

Brocks, Christine. *Die bunte Welt des Krieges: Bildpostkarten aus dem Ersten Weltkrieg 1914-1918.* Essen: Klartext Verlag, 2008.

-----. "Der Krieg auf der Postkarte: Feldpostkarten im ersten Weltkrieg." In *Der Tod als Maschinist: Der industrialisierte Krieg 1914–1918*, eds. Rolf Spilker and Bernd Ulrich, 154-163. Bramsche: Rasch, 1998.

Broun, Heywood. *The A.E.F.: With General Pershing and the American Forces.* New York: D. Appleton, 1918.

Brouwer, Sigmund. *Innocent Heroes: Stories of Animals in the First World War.* Toronto: Tundra Books, 2017.

Brown, Malcolm. *Verdun 1916.* Stroud: Tempus, 2003.

Bruce, J.M. *Nieuport Aircraft of World War One.* London: Arms and Armour Press, 1988.

Bryan, Julien H. *Ambulance 464.* New York: Macmillan, 1918.

Bukowczyk, John J. *A History of Polish Americans.* New Brunswick, NJ: Transaction Publishers, 2008.

Bull, Stephen. *Trench: A History of Trench Warfare on the Western Front.* London: Osprey, 2014.

Bürgschwentner, Joachim. "War Relief, Patriotism and Art: The State-Run Production of Picture Postcards in Austria 1914–1918." *Austrian Studies* 21 (2013), *Cultures at War: Austria-Hungary 1914–1918*: 99-120.

Carlson, Jon D. "Postcards and Propaganda: Postcards as Soft News Images of the Russo-Japanese War." *Political Communication* 26 (2009): 212-237.

Chambers, John Whiteclay II. *To Raise an Army: The Draft Comes to Modern America*. New York: Free Press, 1987.

Chandler, Daniel. *Semiotics: The Basics*, 2nd edition. New York: Routledge, 2007.

Cooper, John Milton, Jr. *Breaking the Heart of the World: Woodrow Wilson and the Fight for the League of Nations*. New York: Cambridge University Press, 2001.

Coppard, George. *With a Machine Gun to Cambrai*. Second Edition. London: Papermac, 1986.

Crowe, James Richard. *Pat Crowe, Aviator: Skylark Views and Letters from France*. New York: N.L. Brown, 1919.

Crutchley, C.E. *Machine Gunner 1914-1918: Personal Experiences of the Machine Gun Corps*. Barnsley: Pen & Sword, 2013.

Danielson, Elena S. "Russian and German Great War Postcards." *Slavic and Eastern European Information Resources* 17, 3 (2016): 151-164.

Dennis, Charles H. *Victor Lawson: His Time and His Work*. Chicago: University of Chicago Press, 1935.

Derren, Marie. "'Entrenched from Life': The Impossible Reintegration of Traumatized French Veterans of the Great War." In: *Psychological Trauma and the Legacies of the First World War*, eds. Jason Crouthamel and Peter Leese, 193-214. London: Palgrave, 2017.

Deutsch, Karl W. *Nationalism and Social Communication: An Inquiry Into the Foundations of Nationality*. Cambridge, MA: MIT Press, 1953.

Deutsches Historisches Museum. *Der Erste Weltkrieg in deutschen Bildpostkarten*, CD-Rom. Berlin: Directmedia Publ., 2004.

de Vries, Guus. *The Great War through Picture Postcards*. Barnsley, England: Pen & Sword Books, 2016.

Dickon, Chris. *The Foreign Burial of American War Dead*. Jefferson, NC: McFarland, 2011.

Dohle, Oskar and Andrea Weiß. "'Österreich wird ewig stehn': Postkarten als Mittel der Propaganda in Österreich-Ungarn im Ersten Weltkrieg am Beispiel der Sammlung des Salzburger Landesarchivs." *Mitteilungen der Gesellschaft für Salzburger Landeskunde* 141 (2001): 293-324.

"Druggist Invents Post-Card Machine." *Dry Goods Reporter* 42, 4 (27 January 1912): 51.

Edwards, Evan Alexander. *From Doniphan to Verdun: The Official History of the 140th Infantry Regiment*. Lawrence, KS: The World Company, 1920.

Ellis, John. *Eye Deep in Hell: Trench Warfare in World War I*. Reprint. Baltimore, MD. John Hopkins University Press, 1989.

Emery, Elizabeth. "The Martyred Cathedral: American Attitudes toward Notre-Dame de Reims During the First World War." In: *Medieval Art and Architecture after the Middle Ages*, eds. Janet T. Marquardt and Alyce A. Jordan, 312-339. Newcastle upon Tyne: Cambridge Scholars Publishing, 2011.

Filloux, Louis. *Miscellaneous Notes Relative to the Materiel of the 155 G.P.F.* N.p., 1917.

Flemming, Thomas and Ulf Heinrich. *Grüße aus dem Schützengraben: Feldpostkarten im Ersten Weltkrieg.* Berlin: be.bra, 2004.

Ford, Nancy Gentile. *Americans All! Foreign-born Soldiers in World War I.* College Station: Texas A&M University Press, 2001.

Franks, Norman. *Nieuport Aces of World War 1.* Oxford: Osprey, 2000.

Fraser, John. "Propaganda on the Picture Postcard." *Oxford Art Journal* 3, 2 (1980), *Propaganda*: 39-47.

Gabler, Neal. *Walt Disney: The Triumph of American Imagination.* New York: Knopf, 2006.

Gale, Tim. *French Army's Tank Force and Armoured Warfare in the Great War.* London/New York: Routledge, 2016.

-----. *French Tanks of the Great War: Development, Tactics and Operations.* Barnsley: Pen & Sword, 2016.

Gallagher, Winifred. *How the Post Office Created America: A History.* New York: Penguin, 2016.

Geyer, Michael. "Rückzug und Zerstörung 1917." In: *Die Deutschen an der Somme 1914-1918: Krieg, Besatzung und verbrannte Erde*, eds. Gerhard Hirschfeld, Gerd Krumeich, and Irina Renz, 163-179. Essen: Klartext, 2006.

Gibbons, Floyd. The Red Knight of Germany: The Story of Baron von Richthofen. San Francisco: Verdun Press, 2014.

Gifford, Daniel. *American Holiday Postcards, 1905-1915: Imagery and Context.* Jefferson, NC: McFarland, 2013.

Glanfield, John. *The Devils' Chariots: The Birth and Secret Battles of the First Tanks.* London: Osprey, 2014.

Gordon, Beverley. "The Souvenir: Messenger of the Extraordinary," *Journal of Popular Culture* 20, 3 (1986): 135-146.

Gottfried, Ted. *George Clemenceau.* New York: Chelsea House, 1987.

Gow, Kenneth. *Letters of a Soldier.* New York: H.B. Covert, 1920.

Greenhalgh, Elizabeth. *Foch in Command: The Forging of a First World War General.* Cambridge/New York: Cambridge University Press, 2011.

Gütgemann-Holtz, Wilma and Wolfgang Holtz, ed. *Neue Photographische Gesellschaft Steglitz: Die Geschichte eines Weltunternehmens.* Berlin: n.p., 2009.

Guttman, Jon. *Caudron G.3.* Berkhamsted, UK: Albatros Publications, 2002.

Hagood, Johnson. *The Services of Supply: A Memoir of the Great War.* Boston: Houghton Mifflin, 1927.

Hallas, James H. *Squandered Victory: The American First Army at St. Mihiel.* Santa Barbara, CA: Praeger, 1995.

Hapak, Joseph T. "Selective Service and Polish Army Recruitment during World War I." *Journal of American Ethnic History* 10, 4 (1991): 38-61.

Works Cited

Harris, Frederick Morgan and William H. Taft, eds., *Service with Fighting Men: An Account of the American Young Men's Christian Associations in the World War*. New York: Association Press, 1922.

Herwig, Holger. *The Marne, 1914: The Opening of World War I and the Battle that Changed the World*. New York: Random House, 2009.

"Historic Postcard Sells for Pounds 27,000." *Times of London*, March 9, 2002.

History of Base Hospital No. 18, American Expeditionary Forces (Johns Hopkins Unit). Baltimore: Base Hospital 18 Association, 1919.

Hobsbawm, Eric. *The Age of Extremes: A History of the World, 1914-1991*. New York: Vintage Books, 1996.

----- and Terence Ranger, eds. *The Invention of Tradition*. Cambridge: Cambridge University Press, 1983.

Hoerner, Ludwig. *Das photographische Gewerbe in Deutschland, 1839-1914*. Düsseldorf: GFW-Verlag, 1989.

Holmes, Richard. *Tommy: The British Soldier on the Western Front, 1914-1918*. London: Harper Perennial, 2004.

Holt, Tonie and Valmai. *Till the Boys Come Home: The First World War Through Its Picture Postcards*, updated edition. Barnsley: Pen and Sword, 2014.

Holzheid, Anett. *Das Medium Postkarte: Eine sprachwissenschaftliche und mediengeschichtliche Studie*. Berlin: Erich Schmidt Verlag, 2011.

Horne, Alistair. *Verdun 1916*. London: Penguin Books, 2007.

Hudson, James J. *In Clouds of Glory: American Airmen Who Flew With the British During the Great War*. Fayetteville: University of Arkansas Press, 1990.

Hüppauf, Bernd. *Fotografie im Krieg*. Paderborn: Wilhelm Fink, 2015.

Huston, James A. *The Sinews of War: Army Logistics, 1775-1953*. Washington: Office of the Chief of Military History, United States Army, 1966.

Hynes, Samuel. *The Unsubstantial Air: American Fliers in the First World War*. New York: Farrar, Straus, & Giroux, 2014.

In memoriam, Albert Craig Funkhouser, Co. F., 144 Inf., 36th Division, Paul Taylor Funkhouser, Co. B., 7th Machine Gun Bn., 3rd Division. Evansville, IN: privately published, 1919.

JBHE Foundation, "'Coon Cards': Racist Postcards Have Become Collectors' Items." *Journal of Blacks in Higher Education 25* (1999): 72-73.

Jessen, Olaf. *Verdun 1916. Urschlacht des Jahrhunderts*. Munich: Beck, 2014.

Joel, Arthur H. *Under the Lorraine Cross*. Charlotte, MI: The Charlotte Tribune, 1921.

Johnson, Ray Neil. *Heaven, Hell, or Hoboken*. Cleveland: O.S. Hubbell, 1919.

Kearns, Séamus. "Picture Postcards As A Source For Social Historians." *Saothar 22* (1997): 128-133.

Keene, Jennifer. *World War I: The American Experience*. Lincoln: University of Nebraska Press, 2011.

Keller, Tait. "Destruction of the Ecosystem." In: *1914-1918-online. International Encyclopedia of the First World War*, ed. by Ute Daniel, Peter Gatrell, Oliver Janz, Heather Jones, Jennifer Keene, Alan Kramer, and Bill Nasson, issued by Freie Universität Berlin, Berlin 2014-10-08. Accessed August 19, 2018. https://encyclopedia.1914-1918-online.net/article/destruction_of_the_ecosystem

Kendall, Paul. *The Zeebrugge Raid 1918: The Finest Feat of Arms*. Stroud: History Press, 2009.

Kennan, George F. *The Decline of Bismarck's European Order: Franco-Russian Relations, 1875-1890*. Princeton, NJ: Princeton University Press, 1979.

Kenny, Kevin. *Making Sense of the Molly Maguires*. New York: Oxford University Press, 1998.

Kimball, Jane. *Trench Art: An Illustrated History*. Davis, CA: Silverpenny Press, 2004.

K. K. Handelsministerium, ed. *Statistik des österreichischen Post- und Telegraphenwesens im Jahre 1914*. Vienna, 1916.

Kocken, Greg. "The Amateur's Eye: Daniel Bastian Nelson in Eau Claire." *Wisconsin Magazine of History* 101, 2 (2018): 29-30.

Lacey, Jim. *Pershing*. New York: Palgrave Macmillan, 2008.

Laffin, John. *World War I in Postcards*. Gloucester: Alan Sutton, 1988.

Larson, E.D.J. *Memoirs of France and the Eighty-eighth Division: Being a Review Without Official Character of the Experiences of the "Cloverleaf" Division in the Great World War from 1917 to 1919*. Minneapolis: privately published, 1920.

Lasusa, Danielle M. "Eiffel Tower Key Chains and Other Pieces of Reality: The Philosophy of Souvenirs." *Philosophic Forum* 38, 3 (2007): 271-287.

Lebeck, Robert and Gerhard Kaufmann. *Viele Grüße...: Eine Kulturgeschichte der Postkarte*. Dortmund: Harenberg, 1985.

Lee, Kennett. *The First Air War, 1914-1918*. New York: Free Press, 1991.

Lengel, Edward. *To Conquer Hell: The Meuse-Argonne, 1918*. New York: Holt, 2008.

Lukan, Walter and Max Demeter Peyfuss. "Jeder Schuß ein Russ', jeder Stoß ein Franzos. Kriegspropaganda auf Postkarten 1914–1918." In *Jeder Schuss ein Russ — Jeder Stoss ein Franzos: Literarische und graphische Kriegspropaganda in Deutschland und Österreich 1914-1918*, eds. Hans Weigel, Walter Lukan and Max Demeter Peyfuss, 32-47. Vienna: Brandstätter, 1983.

Lynch, Charles G., ed. *The Medical Department of the United States Army in the World War*, 17 vols. Washington: GPO, 1921-1929.

Mabry, Gregory. *Recollections of a Recruit: The Official History of the U.S. Fifty-Fourth Infantry*. New York: Schilling, 1919.

MacGaffey, Janet. *Coal Dust On Your Feet: The Rise, Decline, and Restoration of an Anthracite Mining Town*. Lewisburg, PA: Bucknell University Press, 2013.

Marcosson, Isaac F. *S.O.S. America's Miracle in France*. New York: John Lanes, 1919.

Martel, René. *L'Aviation française de bombardement (des origines au 11 novembre 1918)*. Paris: P. Hartmann, 1939.

May, Otto. *Deutsch sein heißt treu sein: Ansichtskarten als Spiegel von Mentalität und Untertanenerziehung in der wilhelminischen Ära (1888–1918)*. Hildesheim: Lax, 1998.

McCarthy, William E. *Memories of the 309th Field Artillery*. Rochester, NT: Henry Conolly, 1920.

McNab, Chris. *The Flamethrower*. London: Bloomsbury, 2015.

Mellinger, Wayne M. "Postcards from the Edge of the Color Line: Images of African Americans in Popular Culture." *Symbolic Interaction* 15, 4 (1992): 413-433.

Miller, Harry W. *Railway Artillery*, 2 vols. Washington, D.C.: Government Printing Office, 1921.

Mooney, James L. *Dictionary of American Naval Fighting Ships*, 8 vols. Washington, D.C.: Navy Department, 1959-1981.

Moore, Ray T. *With the Marines at Belleau Wood: A Vivid Description of Personal Experiences in Battle*. Wake Forest, N.C.: Euzelian Society, 1921.

Morse, Katharine Duncan. *Uncensored Letters of a Canteen Girl*. New York: H. Holt, 1920.

Mosse, George L. *Fallen Soldiers: Reshaping the Memory of the World Wars*. Oxford/New York: Oxford University Press, 1991.

Mroz, Albert. *American Military Vehicles of World War I*. Jefferson, NC: McFarland, 2009.

"Now Appears the Elephant of the Air," *Popular Science Monthly* 92, 4 (April 1918): 528.

"Obituary, Emil C. Kropp." *American Stationer* 63, 1 (1908): 22.

Pencak, William. *For God and Country: The American Legion, 1919-1941*. Boston: Northeastern University Press, 1989.

Pöppinghege, Rainer. *Tiere im Ersten Weltkrieg: Eine Kulturgeschichte*. Berlin: Rotbuch, 2014.

Pottle, Frederick. *Stretchers*. New Haven: Yale University Press, 1929.

Potts, Rolf. *Souvenir*. New York: Bloomsbury, 2018.

Powell, E. Alexander. "A.P.O. 714: The University of the A.E.F." *Scribner's Magazine* 65, 4 (1919): 414.

Prochaska, David and Jordan Mendelson, eds. *Postcards: Ephemeral Histories of Modernity*. University Park, PA: Pennsylvania State University Press, 2010.

Prost, Antoine and Gerd Krumeich. *Verdun 1916: Une histoire franco-allemande de la bataille*. Paris: Talandier, 2015.

Pyta, Wolfram. *Hindenburg: Herrschaft zwischen Hohenzollern und Hitler*. Munich: Siedler, 2007.

Ralphson, G. Harvey. *Over There with the Marines at Chateau Thierry*. Chicago: M.A. Donohue & Co., 1919.

Razac, Oliver. *Barbed Wire: A Political History*. New York: New Press, 2002.

Rogan, Bjarne. "An Entangled Object: The Picture Postcard as Souvenir and Collectible, Exchange and Ritual Communication." *Cultural Analysis* 4 (2005): 1-27.

Rogers, Bob. "Photography and the Photographic Image." *Art Journal* 38, 1 (1978): 29-35.

Roynette, Odile. *Les mots des tranchées: l'invention d'une langue de guerre 1914-1919*. Paris: A. Colin, 2010.

Rüdiger, Ulrike. *Grüsse aus dem Krieg: Die Feldpostkarten aus der Dix-Sammlung Gera*. Gera: Kunstgalerie Gera, 1991.

Rumer, Thomas A. *The American Legion: An Official History*. New York: Evans, 1990.

Ryan, Dorothy B. *Picture Postcards in the United States, 1893-1918*, updated edition. New York: Clarkson N. Potter, 1982.

Sante, Luc. *Folk Photography: The American Real-Photo Postcard*. Portland, OR: Verse Chorus Press, 2009.

Saunders, Nicholas J. *Trench Art*, second edition. Barnsley: Pen & Sword, 2011.

Schubert, Dietrich. "Ein unbekanntes Kriegsbild von Otto Dix: Zur Frage der Abfolge seiner Kriegsarbeiten 1915-1918." *Jahrbuch der Berliner Museen* 38 (1996): 152.

Severn, Mark. *The Gambardier: The Experiences of a Battery of Heavy Artillery on the Western Front During the First World War*. London: Leonaur, 2007.

Shamokin Centennial Committee. *Greater Shamokin Centennial, 1864-1964*. Shamokin, PA: Shamokin Centennial Committee, 1964.

Sharpe, Henry G. *The Quartermaster Corps in the Year 1917 in the World War*. New York: The Century Co., 1921.

Shaver, Arthur L. "Postcarditis Is Now Prevalent." *The Philatelic West* 35, 3 (February 28, 1907): n.p.

Sigel, Lisa Z. "Filth in the Wrong People's Hands: Postcards and the Expansion of Pornography in Britain and the Atlantic World, 1880-1914." *Journal of Social History* 33, 4 (2000): 859-885.

Slotkin, Richard. *Lost Battalions: The Great War and the Crisis of American Nationality*. New York: Holt, 2005.

Smith, Jules A. *In France with the American Expeditionary Forces*. New York: A.H. Hahlo, 1919.

Smucker, John M. *History of the United States Ambulance Service with the French and Italian Armies, 1917-1918-1919*. Allentown, PA: Schlechter, 1967.

Stachelbeck, Christian, ed. *Materialschlachten 1916: Ereignis, Bedeutung, Erinnerung*. Paderborn: Ferdinand Schöningh, 2017.

Stefano, Frank, Jr. *Pictorial Souvenirs and Commemoratives of North America*. New York: E.P. Dutton, 1976.

Striner, Richard. *Woodrow Wilson and World War I: A Burden Too Great to Bear*. Lanham, MD: Rowman & Littlefield, 2014.

Strong, Paul and Sanders Marble. *Artillery in the Great War*. Barnsley: Pen & Sword, 2014.

"Successful Retailer of Postcards." *Dry Goods Reporter*, 42, 21 (May 25, 1912): 40.

Suskind, Richard. *The Battle of Belleau Wood.* New York: Macmillan, 1969.

Terraine, John. *White Heat: The New Warfare 1914-18.* London: Sidgwick & Jackson, 1982.

"The Blockade Runner." *The Fatherland: A Weekly* 5, 3 (August 23, 1916): 48.

United States Army. *Manual for Trench Artillery. Washington, D.C.*: Office of the Adjutant General, 1918.

-----, Center for Military History. *United States Army in the World War, 1917-1919.* Washington: U.S. Army Center for Military History, 1988.

United States Congress, House of Representatives, Select Committee on Expenditures in the War Department. *War Expenditures: Hearings Before Subcommittee No. 3 (Foreign Expenditures)*, Serial 4 – Parts 1-25, vol. 1. Washington: GPO, 1920.

United States War Department. *Historical Report of the Chief Engineer: Including All Operations of the Engineering Department, American Expeditionary Forces, 1917-1919.* Washington: GPO, 1919.

-----. *Location of Graves and Disposition of Bodies of American Soldiers Who Died Overseas.* Washington: Government Printing Office, 1920.

-----. *Organization of the Services of Supply.* Washington: GPO, 1921.

-----. *Report of the Chief of the Motor Transport Corps.* Washington: GPO, 1920.

Van Ells, Mark D. "An Amazing Collection: American GIs and Their Souvenirs of World War II." In *War and Memorials: The Second World War and Beyond*, eds. Frank Jacob and Kenneth Pearl (Paderborn: Ferdinand Schöningh, forthcoming).

Vanderwood, Paul J. "The Picture Postcard as Historical Evidence: Veracruz, 1914." *The Americas* 45, 2 (1988): 210-225.

Vaule, Rosamond B. *As We Were: American Photographic Postcards, 1905-1930.* Boston: David R. Godine, 2004.

von Hagenow, Elisabeth. "Mit Gott für König, Volk und Vaterland: Die Bildpostkarte als Massen- und Bekenntnismedium." In *Bildpropaganda im Ersten Weltkrieg*, ed. Raoul Zühlke, 145-178. Hamburg: Verlag Ingrid Kämpfer, 2000.

Walker, George. *Venereal Diseases in the American Expeditionary Forces.* Baltimore: Medical Standard Book Company, 1922.

Walter, Karin. *Postkarte und Fotografie: Studien zur Massenbild-Produktion.* Würzburg: Bayerische Blätter für Volkskunde, 1995.

Watson, David Robin. *Georges Clemenceau: A Political Biography.* New York: David McKay Company, 1976.

Weingartner, Steven, ed. *Cantigny at Seventy-Five: A Professional Discussion.* Chicago: Robert R. McCormick Tribune Foundation, 1994.

Wictor, Thomas. *German Flamethrower Pioneers of World War I.* Atglen, PA: Schiffer, 2007.

Willoughby, Martin. *A History of Postcards: A Pictorial Record from the Turn of the Century to the Present Day.* London: Bracken Books, 1994.

Witt, Fred Ralph. *Riding to War with "A": A History of Battery A of the 135th Field Artillery.* Cleveland, C. Hauser, 1919.

Wolff, Laetitia, ed. *Real Photo Postcards: Unbelievable Images from the Collection of Harvey Tulcensky.* Princeton, NJ: Princeton Architectural Press, 2005.

Woodward, David R.: *The American Army and the First World War.* New York: Cambridge University Press, 2014.

Yarnell, John. *Barbed Wire Disease: British and German Prisoners of War, 1914-1919* Stroud, England: The History Press, 2011.

Index

240 mm Trench Mortar, 38

A

Aisne-Marne American Cemetery, 63
American Red Cross, 5, 40
American Stationer, xv
Artillery Fire Observers, 41
Austria, x, xi, xv, xix, xxi, xxiv, 4, 5
"avion de chasse", 26

B

Bairnsfather, Bruce, xxviii
Battle of the Somme, xxii
Battle of Verdun, 76, 124
Bausch & Lomb Company of Rochester, xviii
Belgium, xv, 7, 80, 81, 85
Belleau Wood, 62, 63, 78, 83, 84, 93, 101, 102
Berlin, xv
Britain, ix, x, xii, xv, xvi, xviii, xix, xxi, xxii
Britain's Royal Naval Exhibition of 1891, xii
Bulgaria, xix
Burleson, Albert S., xxiii

C

Camp Joseph E. Johnston near Jacksonville, Florida, 6
Camp Pontanezen, 8, 15, 16
Camp Wadsworth, South Carolina, xxx, xxxiv
Caudron, Gaston, 31, 32
Caudron Plane, 31

Caudron, René, 31, 32
Charlton, John P., x
Château-Thierry; 52, 57, 58, 60, 61, 78, 105
Château-Thierry American Monument, 78
Chemin des Dames region, 52, 58
Clemenceau, Georges, 22
"Correspondenz Karte", x
Cummings, E.E., 40
Curt Teich & Company, xv

D

Daily Mail, xxii, xxx
De Rycker & Mendel, xv
Detroit Publishing Company, xv
Dos Passos, John, 40
Doughboy, ix, xxv, xxvii, xxix, xxxv, 8, 9, 12, 13, 14, 16, 17, 58, 87, 97, 120, 121, 127, 129
Dry Good Reporter, xvi

E

Eagle Silk Company, 2, 127
Eastern Front, xix
Eastman Kodak Company of Rochester, xvii
E.C. Kropp Company of Milwaukee, xv
Ernst, Friedrich Wilhelm Victor August, 124
Europe, x, xii, xvii, xviii, xix, xxi, xxii, xxiii, xxix, 2, 3, 7, 63, 118, 126

F

Filloux, Louis Jean François, 42
First World War, v, vi, ix, xv, xviii, xix, xx, xxx, xxxi, xxxiii, 1, 5, 9, 17, 20, 21, 27, 38, 40, 43, 44, 57, 97, 98, 116, 119, 121, 128, 129
France, v, vi, xix, xxi, xxv, xxvi, xxviii, xxix, xxxi, xxxiv, 5, 6, 7, 8, 9, 11, 12, 13, 14, 17, 18, 20, 21, 25, 28, 30, 32, 37, 40, 50, 56, 67, 68, 69, 70, 71, 72, 73, 74, 75, 77, 79, 81 85, 86, 98, 102, 114, 119, 121, 126, 128, 129
Frederick Augustus III, 124
French Canon de 155mm GPF (Grande Puissance Filloux), 42
French Riviera, 13

G

German High Command (*Oberste Heeresleitung*), 122
Germany, vii, xv, xvi, xix, xxi, 5, 13, 20, 29, 32, 50, 118, 122, 124
Greater Shamokin Centennial, 2, 3
Guynemer, Georges, 28, 29

H

Hemingway, Ernest, 40
Hermann, Emanuel, x
Hill 204, 78
Hindenburg, Paul von, 122
Hitler, Adolf, xii, 122
Hook, Theodore, x

I

Italy, xv, xix, xxiii, 1, 40, 85

K

Kluck, Alexander von, 117
Kodak, xvii, xxxiv

L

Langres, 14, 15, 17, 73
Lawson, Victor, xxii
Leighton & Valentine, xv
Lenoncourt, 30, 39
Liersch, Gustav, xv
Lipman, Hymen, x
"Lipman Postal Card", x
Lusitania, xxiii

M

Marhefka, Frank, v, vi, xxxv, 1, 2, 3, 4, 5, 6, 7, 8, 9, 11, 12, 13, 14, 15, 16, 17, 18, 20, 31, 50, 64, 67, 68, 69, 73, 77, 88, 97, 106, 114, 125, 126, 127, 128, 129
mechanized slaughter, xix, 29
Meisner & Buch, xv
Model 3A Folding Pocket Camera, xvii
Montana Peak campaign hat, 82
Moselle River, 60
Motor Supply Train No. 426, 7, 8, 11, 12, 14, 15, 16
Motor Truck Company No. 534, 7
Munk, xv

N

Neue Photographische Gesellschaft, xv
Neufchâteau, 9, 11, 12, 14, 17, 73
Nieuport, 26, 100
North America, xii, 5
Northumberland County coalfields, 1
Norton-Hartjes Ambulance Corps, 40

O

Observation balloons, 34
Old Bill, xxviii
Ottoman Empire, xix

P

Paris, xii, xv, xvii, xxvi, xvii, 20, 21, 24, 25, 35, 41, 44, 50, 51, 52, 58, 61, 63, 98, 102, 111, 114, 116, 118, 119, 121, 127
Pershing, John J., xxiii, 19, 20, 109
Photochrom, xv
Photoglob, xv
Pont-a-Mousson, 60
Pontanezen, 8, 15, 16
Postcard, v, vi, ix, x, xi, xii, xiii, xiv, xv, xvi, xvii, xviii, xix, xx, xxi, xxii, xxiii, xxiv, xxv, xvi, xvii, xviii, xxix, xxx, xxxi, xxxii, xxxiii, xxxiv, xxxv, 1, 14, 16, 17, 18, 20, 31, 50, 56, 58, 63, 64, 68, 73, 88, 89, 97, 100, 102, 112, 114, 123, 125, 126, 128, 129

Q

Queen Victoria, xviii

R

Raphael Tuck & Sons, x, xii, xxi
Reception Park at Bourg, 17, 68
"Red Baron,", 29
Rheims, 64, 80, 88, 89
Richthofen, Manfred von, 29
Russia, x, xix, xxi, 5, 124

S

"saucisse", 34
Services of Supply, 9
Shamokin Dispatch, 127
Shamokin, Pennsylvania, 1
Soissons, 52, 77, 79, 103, 108, 123
Souvenir Post Card Company, xv

Souvenirs, xviii, xxv, xxx, 12, 14, 17, 128, 129
Switzerland, xv

T

Traldi, xv

U

U.S. Post Office, x
U.S.S. *Rambler*, 36, 37, 66
U.S.S. *West Lianga*, 37
United States, v, xi, xiv, xv, xvii, xix, xxiii, xxvi, xxviii, xxxi, 2, 3, 5, 7, 9, 13, 18, 25, 43, 63, 98, 119
United States Army Ambulance Service, 40

V

Veracruz, xxx
Verneuil, 10
Vienne-le- Château, 35
"Vieux Charles", 28
Villa, Pancho, xxxi

W

Walt Disney, 12
Western Civilization, xix
Wilhelm II, 117, 124
Wilson, Woodrow, xxiii, 3, 119
World's Columbian Exposition, xii

Z

Zeebrugge Raid, 94

www.ingramcontent.com/pod-product-compliance
Lightning Source LLC
Chambersburg PA
CBHW052048300426
44117CB00012B/2024